The Grace Walk Experience

STEVE McVEY

HARVEST HOUSE PUBLISHERS

EUGENE, OREGON

Cover by Left Coast Design, Portland, Oregon

Cover photo © Jeremy Walker/The Image Bank/Getty Images

THE GRACE WALK EXPERIENCE

Copyright © 2004 by Steve McVey
Published by Harvest House Publishers
Eugene, Oregon 97402
www.harvesthousepublishers.com
ISBN-13: 978-0-7369-2302-6

Printed in the United States of America

13   14   15   16 / VP-KB / 10   9   8   7   6

Contents

Truth #1
Improving Your Behavior Will Not Give
You Victory in the Christian Life   5

Truth #2
Problems in Your Life Could Be the Best
Thing That Could Happen to You   35

Truth #3
You Must Know Who You Are to
Change What You Do   67

Truth #4
You Don't Have an Evil Twin Living
Inside You.   97

Truth #5
You Can Overcome Temptation by
Understanding Why You Sin   125

Truth #6
Trying to Live by Religious Rules Is the
Surest Way to Live Defeated.   153

Truth #7
God May Be Totally Different from How
You Have Imagined Him to Be   175

Truth #8
Living the Christian Life Can Be Easy   203

Keep Walking!
A Final Word from Steve McVey   238

1

IMPROVING YOUR BEHAVIOR WILL NOT GIVE YOU VICTORY IN THE CHRISTIAN LIFE

Day One

John 10:10

For the next eight weeks we're going to take a journey together. It will be a spiritual journey. We are going to explore some scriptural truths that will transform your life. I know, because that's what happened to me when God began to teach me these things.

For 30 years I tried to live a consistent Christian life. I'm not proud to admit that for 17 of those years I was a local church pastor. I never felt like I was consistent in the way that I wanted to be. My problem wasn't a lack of sincerity. Nobody could have been more serious about their Christian life than I was. Yet I couldn't seem to experience the "abundant life" Jesus talked about in John 10:10. I believed in grace completely, but experiencing it in my own life was often elusive and hard to nail down. I felt frustrated a lot of the time because I knew there had to be more to the Christian life than I was experiencing.

Can you relate to the kind of frustration I'm describing? What would you say are the biggest frustrations you have in trying to live a Christian life? List three of them below.

1. _____

_____

2. _____

_____

3. _____

_____

In 1990, God began to teach me truth that completely revolutionized my life. I'm not exaggerating when I say that when I look back on the person I was before then, it's like I'm looking at somebody else. I certainly don't make any claims to perfection. My family and friends will attest to that. If you knew me well, you'd soon see my short-comings. But I can honestly say that since coming to learn the truths you'll study in this workbook, my life has never been the same. My family and friends will attest to that too.

In the space below, write a short description of what your Christian life would look like if God miraculously answered your prayers about living a victorious life:

_____

_____

_____

_____

_____

_____

_____

Consider what Jesus said in John 10:10: "I came that they might have life, and have it more abundantly." What kind of life did Jesus promise to give us?

John 10:10

_____

What other words would you use as synonyms for "abundant"?

_____

_____

Before we actually begin to look at the eight truths that will enable you to experience the grace walk, it is important for you to understand a vital aspect of your study for these weeks. The biblical truths that will be presented in this study aren't something you can learn. They have to be *revealed* to you by the Holy Spirit. Let me explain.

> *I came that they might have life, and have it more abundantly.*
> *—John 10:10*

There are at least two ways people receive knowledge. Each one has a different effect on us. The first way comes by receiving information. Acquiring content is the goal in this type of learning process. When we learn this way, we come to know something we didn't previously understand.

As we move through these eight weeks together, you will receive content from the Word of God. At the end of this journey, you may find that you possess knowledge of certain scriptural truths you haven't considered until now.

Gaining information can certainly be a good thing. But if that is all that happens in this study, you'll miss the heart of the truths this book communicates. Information will educate you. It will give you knowledge about the subject at hand. However, there is a deeper level of knowledge for those who are Christians. This kind of learning is called *revelation*. It is a higher, more meaningful level of learning because it comes through supernatural means.

Divine revelation occurs when the Holy Spirit takes a truth from the Word of God and causes it to come alive to us so we see it and understand it in a way we have never seen or understood it before. This illumination is one role of the ministry of the Holy Spirit. Jesus promised that Christians have the supernatural capacity to learn spiritual truths. Those who aren't believers don't know anything about this type of learning, because spiritual truths can only be seen by those who are made spiritually alive.

Read 1 Corinthians 2:14 and answer the following question: What difference exists between the way believers and unbelievers comprehend spiritual truth?

1 Corinthians 2:14

_____

_____

In John 16:13, Jesus said that "when He, the Spirit of truth comes, He will guide you into all the truth…" As you begin this journey toward a transformed life, it is important that you approach God's Word with an attitude of dependence on the Holy Spirit. Otherwise, you will miss the deeper element of Bible study.

> *Divine revelation occurs when the Holy Spirit takes a truth from the Word of God and causes it to come alive to us.*

While an education will inform you, revelation from the Word of God will do much more than that. It will *transform* you. It won't just cause you to know more. It will enable you to *be* more as you learn who you are in Christ and how to walk in the power of His indwelling life. That's where the "experience" aspect of the grace walk comes into focus.

John 16:13

That is what I pray takes place for you. Will you pause and pray, asking the Holy Spirit to guide you into all truth as you walk through this study? Ask Him to reveal truth to you that will cause you to be transformed by the supernatural understanding of these eight keys that unlock the door to victory in the Christian life.

Before you pray, pause for a moment and consider the following questions: What do you hope to gain for your life from a study of grace?

_____

_____

How would you briefly describe your concept of grace at this point?

_____

_____

What are the questions for which you would like to find answers from this study?

_____

_____

Tomorrow we'll begin to look at the truths that will cause you to experience the grace walk. First, it's important to lay the right foundation in your heart, isn't it? Would you agree with me in the following prayer? If so, just sign your name to it and date it. You and I are in agreement right now that God will answer this prayer in your life.

Father, give me a revelation of Your grace and transform my life by the full truth of the gospel. I don't want to finish this study with nothing more than a better education in the Bible. I want real transformation in my life. I commit myself to You and look to Your Spirit to guide me into all truth.

Signed: _____

Date: _____

Are you ready to start your journey toward experiencing the grace walk? Good! Let's begin by thinking about how you have lived your Christian life until now. The fact that you are reading a book like this one probably indicates that you have a sincere hunger to live as a victorious Christian. But, if you are like many other Christians, you may feel your level of spiritual victory has been mediocre at best.

Day Two

That is the place that many of us have lived our Christian lives for years. Many know what it is to rededicate themselves to live for God and then to sincerely try hard, only to ultimately discover they just can't live it like they want to.

For some of us, this is all we know of the Christian life. Mediocrity in the Christian life leaves us with a gnawing sense that there *must* be more to being a Christian than this. *Surely,* we think, *this isn't how God means for the Christian life to be!*

The Bible describes the Christian life as joyful and victorious. Maybe, like many others, when you look at the level at which you live as a Christian, it leaves you yearning for something more.

On a scale of one to ten, how well do you experience the following verse in your own life? "Thanks be to God, who always leads us in triumph in Christ" (2 Corinthians 2:14). Pause and think about this question. What numerical value would you assign to your level of victory right now? 1 2 3 4 5 6 7 8 9 10 (circle one). It is important to know where you are before you can discover how to reach where you want to go.

2 Corinthians 2:14

How would you define your Christian walk as you see it at this moment?

☐ *Victorious always*

☐ *Occasional victories, occasional defeats*

☐ *More defeats than victories*

☐ *Not as good as I could be, but not as bad as some others*

☐ *Defeated*

Do you truly believe it is possible to live a victorious Christian life? Or do you believe you will always be defeated? Be honest about your answer.

For the remainder of this week, we are going to examine the first biblical truth that can help you experience this grace walk. Read it slowly and meditate on this first truth. If you struggle over whether it is true or not, that's okay. As you move through this week of study, I will offer biblical evidence to persuade you.

Truth #1: Improving your behavior will not give you victory in the Christian life.

At first glance, this statement may sound *untrue* to you. After all, most of us have even heard in church that we should rededicate ourselves to God to do better. On the surface, it sounds right, but I want to ask you a question about your own experience: Has trying to improve your behavior given you victory in the Christian life?

It has often been said that the definition of insanity is doing the same thing in the same way time and time again and expecting different results. We will come to scriptural evidence of this truth later, but for now consider what you've seen in your own life. While it's true that personal experience isn't the final authority in determining spiritual truth, we can't ignore the reality of our experiences either.

> Truth #1: Improving your behavior will not give you victory in the Christian life.

Have you sincerely tried your best to achieve the victorious Christian life? Stop for a moment and identify the ways you have tried to become a victorious Christian. What are some of the things you've done to try to be victorious?

_____

_____

_____

_____

Now I want you to be honest in answering this question: How long did your efforts last in enabling you to experience victory? I understand. That's how it worked for me too when I believed that victory was the result of my "commitment." Time and time again, my commitment fizzled and I found myself right back at the place of inconsistency and defeat.

There is a Bible word for this kind of approach to Christian living. It is the word *flesh*. It is a way of life that comes from sheer willpower. A flesh walk often revolves around promising God that we will do better, and then trying with all our hearts to do it—only to fail again.

This approach simply won't work. It doesn't work because it isn't God's way. His plan isn't that we should try harder to have victory, but that we should *trust Him.* I want us to build on this life-changing principle for the rest of the week and allow the Holy Spirit to reveal this truth to us from the Word of God. We will start with the foundation, then build on it a layer at a time.

Let's begin by recognizing there are two ways for a person to live his life. To do that, we're going to contrast what I call "the flesh walk" and "the grace walk." These two are in diametrical opposition to each other.

The flesh walk stresses dedicating ourselves to live for God. When I use the term *flesh*, don't limit your understanding of the word to the worst behaviors—like drugs, drunkenness, immorality—the really bad-looking things. Living in the flesh sometimes leads to those kinds of activities, but it doesn't have to look like that.

To walk after the flesh really just means living out of our own abilities. Another way to describe it is *self-sufficiency. Flesh* refers to those techniques I depend on when I try to get my needs met or manage my own life apart from Jesus Christ.

It is important to understand that walking after the flesh doesn't have to look disgusting or be what you would define as "bad." In fact, the flesh walk can look pretty good to others. My own flesh patterns have primarily been what might be called "religious flesh." Most people haven't known when I've walked after my flesh because it looked pretty good to them. I'm sure I'm not the only one who has had this kind of flesh.

Maybe you do too. If you've grown up in church, there is a good chance that this is the case. We're not alone in this place. The apostle Paul was another person who had religious-looking flesh.

Read Philippians 3:3-6 and consider his description of his own brand of flesh:

Philippians 3:3-6

> *We are the true circumcision, who worship in the Spirit of God and glory in Christ Jesus and put no confidence in the flesh, although I myself might have confidence even in the flesh. If anyone else has a mind to put confidence in the flesh, I far more: circumcised the eighth day, of the nation of Israel, of the tribe of Benjamin, a Hebrew of Hebrews; as to the Law, a Pharisee; as to zeal, a persecutor of the church; as to the righteousness which is in the Law, found blameless.*

Highlight or underline the word *flesh* each time Paul uses it.

What are the two types of individuals that Paul contrasts?

   1. Those who put _____ in the flesh.

   2. Those who put no _____ in the flesh.

Is there an "in between" group?

Do you agree that Paul is saying either you *do* put confidence in the flesh or you *do not* put confidence in the flesh? Yes or no?

Bracket the phrases Paul uses to describe his flesh. What contemporary phrases would you use in place of his that basically mean the same thing?

Paul called it:	Today we might say:

Paul's behavior looked pretty good to other people, but it was all flesh. It was the way he tried to earn favor with God—doing the best he knew to do what he thought God wanted him to do. He was a long way off base, wouldn't you agree?

So it is possible, then, to sincerely be trying to do what we think God wants and still miss the mark. Even if we could improve our actions, it might be nothing more than improving our flesh, which would get us nowhere further toward experiencing the grace walk.

End your study today making sure you understand the meaning of *flesh*. How have we defined *flesh* in this study?

Flesh means living out of _____ .

Another way to describe it is

_____ — _____ .

We have seen that it is possible to be sincerely trying to do what we think God wants and still be walking after the flesh. You can try to live for Jesus and miss the mark altogether. As strange as it might seem right now, *trying* to live for Christ can be based in a legalistic paradigm. Grace is about *trusting*, not trying.

Day Three

Law and grace are two systems of living in this world that are in total opposition to each other. One cancels the other out. We are either living out of God's grace or living in legalism. It can't be both ways.

Where did the idea originate that we can achieve spiritual victory by trying harder? To answer that question, we have to go all the way back to the Garden of Eden. Consider Genesis 2:8-9:

Genesis 2:8-9

> The LORD God planted a garden toward the east, in Eden; and there He placed the man whom He had formed. Out of the ground the LORD God caused to grow every tree that is pleasing to the sight and good for food; the tree of life also in the midst of the garden, and the tree of the knowledge of good and evil.

At the very beginning, God set two trees in the midst of the garden that He had created for mankind. These two trees represent the two ways of living that we may choose. What are these two trees?

1. _____

2. _____

One of these trees revolves around self-improvement. The other is grounded in supernatural transformation. These two trees are the *tree of life* and the *tree of the knowledge of good and evil.*

The Trusting Tree

What do these two trees represent? The tree of life represents Jesus Christ. How can we know that? By interpreting the Old Testament in light of the New Testament. Even a casual reading of the New Testament reveals that when the Bible talks about life, it is pointing us to Jesus. He is the source of life.

Read the following statements from the New Testament. In each, underline or highlight the word *life* and the word *Jesus* (or the word that indicates Jesus).

- *"When Christ, who is our life, is revealed, then you also will be revealed with Him in glory" (Colossians 3:3-4).*

- *"I am the resurrection and the life" (John 11:25).*

- *"I am the way, and the truth, and the life" (John 14:6).*

- *"In Him was life" (John 1:4).*

How does the New Testament define *life?*

Colossians 3:3-4

John 11:25

John 14:6

John 1:4

The tree of life, then, represents Jesus Christ. Any man who lives from this tree will live in union with God forever, being one with Him. Life flows from Christ, and those who live in Him have life. It's that simple. John 3:36 says that "he who believes in the Son has eternal life." Why? Because they are living from the tree of life, *which is Christ.*

John 3:36

God wants you to live from that tree (Jesus) every day, allowing His life to flow through you in the same way that the life of a fruit tree flows into the fruit itself. When Adam ate from the tree of the knowledge of good and evil, he led mankind on a different path. But Jesus Christ came to correct the damage and undo the harm that Adam had done.

The Trying Tree

However, another tree stood in the garden. It was the tree of the knowledge of good and evil. This tree pictures the system of law. Look at its name again: the tree of the knowledge of *good* and *evil,* or *right* and *wrong.* In what way did this tree give knowledge? It gave the knowledge of right and wrong. It is the tree of morals, the tree of law.

Consider what God said about that tree in Genesis 2:16-17:

Genesis 2:16-17

> *The Lord God commanded the man, saying, "From any tree of the garden you may eat freely; but from the tree of the knowledge of good and evil you shall not eat, for in the day that you eat from it you will surely die."*

The law tree is all about doing—do this, don't do that—you must do this, you must do that. What did God instruct about Adam and Eve's relationship to that tree?

God said, "Do not eat from that tree. If you do, you will certainly die."

The tree of the knowledge of good and evil could also be called the *rules* tree. The tree of life was the *relationship* tree. The tree of the knowledge of good and evil was about *trying*. The tree of life was about *trusting*. Do you see the difference?

It is not God's intent that man should live by the law tree, but rather by the life tree. Don't misunderstand and think I'm suggesting behavior isn't important. It is. The issue at hand here is *how* our behavior is established.

God intends for you to experience victory in your Christian walk by trusting, not by trying. You may have tried to improve yourself to become victorious, but God never asked you to do that. He only asks that you trust Him and let Him transform you. But if you keep taking the same wrong approach you've always taken, you'll get the same defeating results.

Look further at the Genesis account. The serpent came to Eve, and he told her a lie about the tree of the knowledge of good and evil. Genesis 3:5 quotes the serpent:

> *"God knows that in the day you eat from it your eyes will be opened, and you will be like God, knowing good and evil."*

Genesis 3:5

What lie does the serpent tell Eve about the tree? Underline the lie in his statement.

The serpent tells her this lie: "If you eat from the tree of the knowledge of good and evil, you will be like God." The lie was that there was something she could *do* to become more godlike. A second lie is hidden under the surface of this statement. "You will be like God," the serpent said. In reality, Eve was already like God. The serpent implied that she was not like God, but by eating of the tree of the knowledge of good and evil, she could become like God:

> *Then God said, "Let Us make man in Our image, according to Our likeness"…God created man in His own image, in the image of God He created him; male and female He created them… God saw all that He had made, and behold, it was very good"* *(Genesis 1:26-31).*

Genesis 1:26-31

This passage teaches that God had already made Adam and Eve like Him. They were created in His own image. But the serpent comes to Eve and he says, "Do you want to be more like God? Let me tell you something you can *do*."

The first lie in Scripture is told right here. The lie was, "If you do this thing, then you'll be more like God." But they were already like God. The serpent made them think they were deficient in some way, but they weren't.

> What will become very clear ...is this: You are already Christlike.

I must admit that for many of the years I served as a local church pastor, I taught that same lie to my congregation. I said, "You want to be like Christ? Here's what you do." There was one big difference between the serpent and me. He only gave them one thing to do. I gave them a thousand! I put them on the "try harder treadmill" every Sunday.

I gave them lists of things they could do, steps they could take toward becoming more Christlike by improving their behavior. But what will become very clear to you as you move through this study is this: *You are already Christlike.*

When we live from the law tree, we find ourselves constantly trying to do something that God has already done. If God has already done all that is necessary for us to experience victory, then trying harder won't accomplish anything except to create a greater sense of frustration! Watchman Nee once described it this way: "Oh, the folly of trying to enter a room that you're already in."

In your imagination, take a step back and look into your life as if you were an all-seeing observer. As the observer, you can see what you do and why you do it. What do you see yourself doing because you think it will make you more like Christ?

Some things I have done to try to improve and be more like Christ are:

Did these things work? Are you beginning to see that improving your behavior is not the need in your life? The need each of us have rests in Jesus, not in ourselves and what we do.

Day Four

Genesis 3:7

Are you beginning to see from our study of the two trees in the Garden of Eden that to try to achieve spiritual victory by improving our behavior won't work? It isn't the way God has designed for us to experience victory in the Christian life. The very idea of experiencing grace by *trying* is a contradiction. Grace is *received, not achieved.*

No matter how sincere we are or how hard we try, God is not going to allow us to succeed in living the Christian life by our own fleshly determination.

When Adam and Eve saw their nakedness, they concluded, "Something is wrong with us! We aren't presentable to God like this!" Consequently, they set out by their own efforts to make themselves more acceptable to God. Read Genesis 3:7 and note what they did to try to improve their appearance before God:

_____

They thought they had to improve themselves to be okay with God. That's what legalism still causes people to believe today. A person who is trapped in legalism examines himself, determines he is not good enough like he is, and goes out and tries to do something by his own efforts to make himself presentable to God.

The irony of Adam and Eve's self-improvement plan was that they were *already* fine with God. He had seen them naked from the day they were created, but the "legalism tree" caused them to think they needed to do something to improve themselves.

So here is where it all began—in the Garden of Eden. It was when Adam and Eve ate from the *forbidden* tree that man began to focus on improving his behavior as a way to experience a victorious life. Do you see how this first truth is directly linked to disobedience in

IMPROVING YOUR BEHAVIOR WILL NOT GIVE YOU VICTORY IN THE CHRISTIAN LIFE

the Garden of Eden? Improving your behavior will *not* give you victory in the Christian life, because to take that route is to live from the wrong tree!

As you consider each of these consequences, how do you see them manifested in your own life? What we need is not a change in behavior. What we need is a change in our attitude about our life source. We need to experience living out of the life of Jesus Christ. That's what Christianity is.

Read the complete text in Genesis chapters 2-3. There are at least two other consequences associated with eating from that tree that have to do with trying to improve ourselves. They are:

1. Being self-conscious about how God sees us.

2. Trying to build our lives around the right values.

Highlight the verses in your Bible that demonstrate the two consequences listed above. What is the evidence that these two consequences existed in Adam and Eve's lives? Write a short paragraph describing how these two characteristics have affected your own life since you have been a Christian.

_____

_____

_____

_____

Improving your behavior will not *give you victory in the Christian life, because to take that route is to live from the wrong tree!*

Genesis 2-3

THE GRACE WALK EXPERIENCE   25

To what extent has the tree of the knowledge of good and evil influenced the modern church today? Are there ways that contemporary Christianity encourages people to eat from this tree that God said not to touch? If so, in what ways does that happen?

_____

_____

_____

_____

_____

_____

_____

_____

_____

_____

The flesh walk is a performance-based lifestyle. It's the idea I must improve myself in order to be a good Christian. The focus is on performance more than it is on the person of Jesus Christ.

I'm not minimizing the place of Christian service or the importance of behavior. I'm simply suggesting that in the modern church we often have it backward. We think, *If I can just behave in a certain way, if I can just do certain things, then I could become godly. Then I could become Christlike.* That is a legalistic mind-set. The Bible teaches that when we know we are Christlike because of what He has done in us and through us, the knowledge of *that* truth is what will change our behavior.

Day Five

A person who is living out of the law tree is walking after the flesh, living out of his own self-sufficiency. He thinks that somehow there's something he can do that will enable him to experience victory himself.

He imagines God wants him to change himself, even *needs* him to improve. In fact, some even think that God *needs* them to serve Him. God needing us? This is the God who stood on the edge of nothingness and said, "Let there be"—and there was. What could we possibly have that He needs?

Have you believed that God needs you? If so, I challenge you to make a list of the things you have that you think God might need. Then you take that paper and step up to the boundary between time and eternity and say to God, "Here, God. Here are some things I think you might need!" I don't think you can bring yourself to do it.

God doesn't need us. But far better than that, He wants us. Imagine if I said to my wife, "Honey, I really need you. After all, who would

I have to cook for me? Or who would iron my shirts? Or take care of the household? I really need you." You see, it's better than that. I *want* my wife. And so God wants you.

Acts 17:24-28

Read Acts 17:24-28. As you read thoughtfully, look for this: At a certain place, Paul moves from talking about the God who *does not need*…to talking about the God who *wants*. Identify the two perfectly compatible aspects of who God is.

> *The God who made the world and all things in it, since He is Lord of heaven and earth, does not dwell in temples made with hands; nor is He served by human hands, as though He needed anything, since He Himself gives to all people life and breath and all things; and He made from one man every nation of mankind to live on all the face of the earth, having determined their appointed times and the boundaries of their habitation, that they would seek God, if perhaps they might grope for Him and find Him, though He is not far from each one of us; for in Him we live and move and exist.*

Stop reading for a moment and consider with both heart and mind what it means to you that God *wants* you. Think about everything He has done to save you only because He wants you. When you had no interest in any kind of self-improvement, He forgave you and brought you into His family! (Read Romans 5:8.)

Roman 5:8

Do you really think that, if He was willing to accept you when you were a filthy sinner, He now has His arms crossed and is impatiently waiting for you to improve? No! It was His job to save you, and He alone assumes the role of sanctifying you too. Your role is to simply trust Him. Faith, alone, is the key to salvation and faith, alone, is the key to transformation in your life.

We will never be able to understand the victorious Christian life and the abundance promised in Scripture until we realize that fact. God isn't waiting for us to change ourselves. He loves and wants us as His bride. When we become consumed with the union we share with Him, we won't stop serving Him even if it costs our very lives. The transformation we long to know will come then, but it won't be because of our own determination. He will bring it about in us.

On the other hand, if we don't understand the union—the identity that we have *in* Christ—then we will struggle under the power of our flesh, trying to do things that will bring us victory, instead of simply trusting God to be who He is in us.

There are certain characteristics of the flesh walk that are very common. Examine your own lifestyle in light of these and see if they fit you. If so, that fact is evidence you are still attempting to live from your own ability.

God isn't waiting for us to change ourselves. He loves and wants us as His bride.

Reputation

When a person is living from the law tree, how he looks to other people is of utmost importance. He absolutely must make a good impression. People have to think well of him. His personal sense of value depends on it. Consider the contrast between that attitude and the one of Jesus, who the Bible says made Himself of no reputation (see Philippians 2:7 KJV).

Philippians 2:7

In what ways have you tried to make a good impression on other people?

_____

Accomplishments

A second characteristic of the flesh walk is an obsession with measurable accomplishments. What can I do? What can I achieve? To one who is consumed with the need for self-improvement, accomplishments are necessary to validate him as an individual of worth. Without them, he can't be sure of his true value.

Have you tried to gain your sense of value from your accomplishments? In what ways do you see this to be the case in your life?

_____

Positive Self-Image

This is of primary concern to one who is enslaved to the insatiable quest for perfection. He needs to feel good about himself at all costs. To the legalistic Christian, imperfection in his life is not an option. He can never rest, because he is always tweaking his performance in a futile attempt to see himself in the best possible light.

_____

When Adam and Eve ate from the tree of the knowledge of good and evil, man was left to his flesh until Jesus redeemed us. But along the way, there were those who trusted in God instead of trusting in their own self-sufficiency. Their focus wasn't so much on what they did as on who they were in relation to God.

In God's kingdom, your value is not in what you do. The flesh walk stresses trying to build an identity through what you do. But the essence of the grace walk is abiding in Jesus Christ.

Read through the following verses from the Gospel of John. At the end of each verse, answer the following question: What was the source of Jesus' life and power?

- *"I can do nothing on My own initiative" (John 5:30).*

- *"My teaching is not Mine, but His who sent Me" (John 7:16).*

- *"I do nothing on My own initiative, but I speak these things as the Father taught Me" (John 8:28).*

- *"I have not even come on My own initiative, but He sent Me" (John 8:42).*

- *"I did not speak on My own initiative, but the Father Himself who sent Me has given Me a commandment as to what to say and what to speak" (John 12:49).*

- *"The word which you hear is not Mine, but the Father's who sent Me" (John 14:24).*

John 5:30

John 7:16

John 8:28

John 8:42

John 12:49

John 14:24

What is the source that provided His life, His action in the world?

_____

Jesus didn't do things for God. He trusted God to live His life through the Son. God was the source of His life.

The early church understood this fact. Peter said it like this on the Day of Pentecost:

Acts 2:22

Men of Israel, listen to these words: Jesus the Nazarene, a man attested to you by God with miracles and wonders and signs which God performed through Him in your midst, just as you yourselves know (Acts 2:22).

God acted through Jesus. Jesus never acted independently, but always trusted the Father to act through Him.

John 20:21

How are we to relate to Jesus? We are to relate to Jesus in the same way that Jesus related to the Father. "Jesus said to them again, 'Peace be with you; as the Father has sent Me, I also send you'" (John 20:21). In other words, "In the same way I went out, you go out. Just as I trusted in the Father, You trust in Me."

John 15:5

In John 15:5 He said,

I am the vine, you are the branches; he who abides in Me and I in him, he bears much fruit, for apart from Me you can do nothing (John 15:5).

Consider this question: How many miracles could Jesus have done if He had acted independently? _____ The answer will be given in the next few paragraphs.

Jesus is, was, and always has been God. He was God when He was in this world. But, even though He was God, He chose not to live out of His deity, but to live out of His humanity. Don't misunderstand this point. I am not suggesting that Jesus was not God while He was on earth. He was God. He has always been God. But He emptied

Philippians 2:7

Himself (Philippians 2:7) of divine prerogatives and lived as a man.

He laid aside the rights associated with His deity and at every moment, while on earth, lived out of His humanity. We know Him as the Son of God. But when you read the Gospels, He never referred to Himself as the Son of God. He referred to Himself as the Son of Man. He lived in this world as a man who depended entirely on God to be His life. Nothing He did originated from Himself. Everything He did was the life of God pouring out of Him.

The answer to the question about how many miracles Jesus would have done on His own is *none*. How do we know that Jesus could have done no miracles had He not depended on God to act through Him? It's because of what He said about the matter:

> *Truly, truly, I say to you, the Son can do nothing of Himself, unless it is something He sees the Father doing; for whatever the Father does, these things the Son also does in like manner (John 5:19).*

What can we accomplish when we don't trust Christ to live through us? Nothing. You and I are to go out into the world understanding the union we have with Christ. And when we do that, Jesus said that rivers of living water would come flowing out of our innermost being (see John 7:38). You don't have to pump it up. It will come flowing out when you trust Jesus as your very life.

Legalism says you have to do certain things to improve yourself as a Christian. Grace says, "Just be who you are in Christ and watch rivers of living water come flowing out of your innermost being." When you are abiding in Jesus Christ, supernatural works of God through love, mercy, compassion, will come pouring out of you.

As you abide in Christ, rivers of living water will come flowing out of you, and everyone around you is going to get soaking wet with the love and life of God. It isn't up to you to try harder to improve, but

> *What can we accomplish when we don't trust Christ to live through us? Nothing.*

John 5:19

John 7:38

to trust Christ to be who He is in you and through you as you live your daily routine.

As you come to the end of this week's study, consider what you have learned about the difference between legalism and grace. Beside each word, write "L" for law or "G" for grace.

☐	*performance*	☐	*trusting*
☐	*behavior*	☐	*personality*
☐	*being*	☐	*trying*
☐	*flesh*	☐	life of Christ

This first truth is foundational in having your life transformed. Improving your behavior will not give you victory in the Christian life. Accept this truth and ask the Holy Spirit to guide you forward into the next truth along your pathway to victorious Christian living.

2

Problems in Your Life Could Be the Best Thing That Could Happen to You

John 10:10

Day One

The truth we will consider this week is the bridge that carries us from the place where we are constantly trying to improve ourselves in order to experience victory, to the place where we live each day enjoying the abundant life that Jesus promised (see John 10:10). The subject matter of this truth may seem negative to you, but it isn't a negative subject when we see it from God's perspective. According to at least one passage in Scripture (which we will consider tomorrow), problems give us a reason to rejoice.

Last week we learned that trying to improve ourselves through self-effort can never lead to victorious living. As you progress through this book, you will discover that each of the truths in this study link together to carry you forward in your journey toward experiencing the grace walk. Your goal is personal transformation, which is good because that's God's goal for you too.

Review a few of the important aspects of the truth considered last week. Your understanding of that truth is a building block upon which the truth we will consider this week stands.

In your own words, briefly describe the difference between grace and law.

_____

_____

What is your understanding of the word *flesh?*

_____

_____

What are the two branches on the law tree?

_____

_____

How can behavior that looks good or right still be flesh?

_____

_____

What is the problem with trying to improve our behavior to reach the place of victorious Christian living?

_____

_____

The flesh walk, at best, is a mediocre life. But to walk in grace is to allow Jesus Christ to live His life through us so we live beyond our own natural capabilities. We live by the life of Another. When we do that, we experience more than moral living. We experience miraculous living because Christ lives through us.

The Doorway to Experiencing the Grace Walk

You might be thinking, *That sounds good. It would be wonderful to live in such a way that Christ is expressing His life through me. But how do I live that life? How do I get to that place?* In the weeks ahead, you will learn some biblical, theological truth that will help you to understand how you are to live that life, but for this week's study I want to share with you what I believe is the entrance way into victorious living.

This is the doorway through which every person must pass who wants to experience the life of Christ being expressed in and through him. There is no avoiding this. This entrance through which we must pass is the doorway of brokenness.

Brokenness is a condition that exists when a person has given up all confidence in his own ability to manage life.

It would be wise for you to memorize that definition of brokenness. It is the foundation for this week's study. How does God bring us to the place of brokenness? The thing He often uses to bring us to that point is suffering.

> *Brokenness is a condition that exists when a person has given up all confidence in his own ability to manage life.*

The modern church has varied opinions about suffering in the life of a Christian. Some teach that, as believers, we are never to suffer. Those who teach that error need to go back and examine what the Bible says about the matter because it clearly speaks of the reality of suffering in our lives, whether we are believers or not. Every person who lives in this world is going to experience suffering.

What is your understanding of the role of suffering in a Christian's life? How has the teaching you have received caused you to view suffering? Write "T" or "F" for the following True/False statements.

1. *If I have enough faith, bad things will not happen in my life.*

2. *When bad things happen, it is always because there is sin in my life.*

3. *If I follow Christ, many bad things will happen because Satan will attack me.*

4. *When God allows suffering in my life, it is because He can use it for His redemptive purposes to set me free from my self-sufficiency and cause me to live in grace.*

(The first three statements are false and the last one is true.)

Jesus spoke to this issue by addressing the need for brokenness in our lives in John 12:24:

> *Unless a grain of wheat falls into the earth and dies, it remains alone; but if it dies, it bears much fruit.*

John 12:24

What was Jesus talking about here? He was letting us know that in order to follow Him we must die to our own life and embrace His. In fact, in the very next verse he says if we struggle to hold onto life, we will lose it. But if we are willing to let go of our lives in order to experience His, we will find life in the fullest sense of the word.

To bring us to the place where we see the futility of trying to hold on to our own life, God will allow problems to come that shake our sense of self-security. He uses troubles in our lives to get our attention. Then He shows us how to embrace real life.

I'll tell you how it is. Have you ever seen an excerpt from the old television program *The Ed Sullivan Show* in which a man would take a long rod, about 10 or 12 feet tall, and put a plate on the end of the rod and spin the plate? Then he would stick the rod in the air with the plate spinning on it. He'd shake the rod to keep the plate spinning. Then he'd get another rod and put another plate on it and get that plate spinning and put the rod up. Then he'd go back to the first rod and shake it to keep the plate spinning. Then he'd shake the second rod to kept that plate spinning. Then he'd get a third rod and repeat the process. He'd keep on until he had ten or twelve rods with plates spinning on all of them and he would run back and forth, shaking rods to keep the plates spinning. Back and forth, back and forth, back and forth. He'd keep all the plates spinning. That's what our Christian lives look like when we're operating out of the flesh.

Do you know what happens? God looks at you and says, "I love you too much to let you spend your life that way." So, in His love and kindness, He comes walking across the stage of life knocking all your plates off. One after another, He knocks your plates off.

> God looks at us and says, "I love you too much to let you spend your life that way."

It's kind of funny to watch how the body of Christ responds to that experience. The Baptists all go to church the next Sunday to walk the aisle and rededicate their lives to try harder to keep their plates in the air. The Pentecostals begin to renounce the demon of plate-breaking. The Charismatics lay their hands on the plate and say, "In Jesus' name, be healed." The Methodists appoint a committee to conduct a yearlong study of the plate breaking and to determine whether it was actually wrong, or was simply the predisposition of the plate from the time it was manufactured. The Presbyterians say the plate was preordained to break from the foundation of the world. And the Salvation Army says, "You know, when you really stop to think about it, aren't we really all broken plates?"

I hope you recognize my sense of humor. I'm not really making fun of anybody. I'm just pointing out the one thing we all have in common. We don't want to recognize that it's really God knocking those plates off. God uses suffering to expose our flesh patterns.

Name the "spinning plates" in your life.

_____

_____

_____

Describe what you have to do to keep them spinning.

_____

_____

_____

Has God been knocking any plates off? Describe what He has been doing.

In tomorrow's lesson you will begin your discovery of how God uses suffering to bring you into a life of victory. As you begin this first day of study in a new week, will you pray right now and ask the Holy Spirit to guide you into the revelation of the value of suffering in your life? Don't waste the painful circumstances of life. God wants to use them to accomplish a wonderful purpose in you.

1 Peter 4:12-13

Yesterday we learned that Jesus had something to say about the importance of suffering. The apostle Peter had a word on the matter too. He wrote to the church in 1 Peter 4:12-13, saying,

> *Beloved, do not be surprised at the fiery ordeal among you, which comes upon you for your testing, as though some strange thing were happening to you; but to the degree that you share the sufferings of Christ, keep on rejoicing, so that also at the revelation of His glory you may rejoice with exultation.*

Underline the phrase "at the revelation of His glory." Think about what it means. At the revelation of His glory you will rejoice with *exultation*—unbridled, exuberant enthusiasm. Joy that can't be contained, being absolutely thrilled.

I used to read that and think, *Wow! Is that kind of joy possible? Well, when does it happen?* And then I saw "at the revelation of His glory," and in my feeble, pathetic, anemic standard of Christian living, I said, "That must be talking about when we get to heaven. Nobody could have that kind of joy down here." But that's not what Peter is talking about.

What is "the revelation of His glory"? Paul answers this way: "Christ in you, the hope of glory." The revelation of His glory is when you realize the full riches of Christ in you. It is when you come to understand your identity in Jesus Christ. The tool that God often uses to bring us to that place where we know who we are in Christ is suffering. Suffering will often bring one to brokenness.

Pain Is a Normal Part of Living

Maybe sometimes you've wondered, *Why do I have to suffer? Why does God allow suffering?* We need to realize that suffering is a universal condition. All humans experience suffering. Do you want to know what you did to experience suffering? I'll tell you—you were born. And because you were born, now you're going to suffer. It goes with the territory where you live here on planet Earth.

Job 5:7 tells us, "A man is born for trouble as sparks fly upward." In Job 14:1 the Bible says, "Man, who is born of woman, is short-lived and full of turmoil." Jesus Himself said, "In the world you have tribulation" (John 16:33). Suffering is the condition of all humanity. It is universal.

Don't think that believers are exempt from painful events in life, because they are not. It bothers me in the modern church that there are those who teach that pain is not an authentic part of the lives of those who are walking in faith. These "artificial joy boys" who suggest that if you suffer, then your faith must be weak, need to go back to their Bibles. They need to teach and preach what is true rather than what they wish were true. Because of that kind of faulty teaching, a lot of Christians who have suffered have been made to feel guilty about their suffering. Some of the greatest people of God through the ages have been people who know what it means to suffer.

Today we will consider such a man. His name was Job. I don't need to tell you about the righteousness of Job. You already know what a godly man he was. His life was so pure that God used Job as an exhibit of righteousness.

> *Don't think that believers are exempt from painful events in life, because they are not.*

Job 5:7
Job 14:1
John 16:33

Job 1:8

Have you considered My servant Job? For there is no one like him on the earth, a blameless and upright man, fearing God and turning away from evil (Job 1:8).

God said these words to Satan himself.

Job 23:1-10

Let's consider Job's encounter with suffering. He writes about his situation in Job 23:1-10.

Even today my complaint is bitter;
his hand is heavy in spite of my groaning.
If only I knew where to find him;
if only I could go to his dwelling!
I would state my case before him
and fill my mouth with arguments.
I would find out what he would answer me,
and consider what he would say.
Would he oppose me with great power?
No, he would not press charges against me.
There an upright man could present his case before him,
and I would be delivered forever from my judge.
But if I go to the east, he is not there;
if I go to the west, I do not find him.
When he is at work in the north, I do not see him;
when he turns to the south, I catch no glimpse of him.
But he knows the way that I take;
when he has tested me, I will come forth as gold (NIV).

Summarize what Job is feeling in your own words.

_____

_____

_____

_____

_____

Identify (by underlining) in the above passage where Job was saying the following:

1. God seems to be against me right now.

2. God seems to be hiding from me at a time when I need Him most.

3. If only I could make sense of my situation, I could more easily bear it.

Does it sound to you like Job knew what it was to suffer? We know Job was a godly man. The Bible tells us Job never sinned with his lips. He never sinned through this trial and his response to it. Look at the response of this godly man.

Job Felt Like God Was Against Him

Job described how he felt: "His hand is heavy in spite of my groaning" (Job 23:2 NIV). This description of the heavy hand of God pictures a man with his face in the dirt. He's trying to push himself up, but there's a hand that keeps pushing him back into the mud again. Job said, "That's how I feel. The heavy hand of God is on me, pushing me down into the dirt." It seemed God was against him. Have you ever felt that way?

Job 23:2

He Felt Despair Because His Troubles Made No Sense to Him

Note Job's sense of despair in verse 3: "If only I knew where to find him; if only I could go to his dwelling!" (NIV). He's saying, "Where is God? I wish I knew where I could find God." His words indicated

Job 23:3

his feelings—"If I could just understand it, I could endure it." How many times during a trial have we said, "If I could just make sense of it. If I could just see the purpose." Job knew what that was like. His circumstances made no sense to him at all. He said, "If I could find Him, I could approach Him and ask Him. I could plead with Him to make me understand what's happening here."

Have you ever been at that place where your circumstances made no sense at all? To Job it seemed that God was hiding just when Job needed Him most. In verses 8 and 9 he describes his search. It's like he's saying,

Job 23:8-9

> *Every time I think I know where to look, I look and He's not there. I look everywhere for God, but He is nowhere. At the time I need God most, He's nowhere to be found.*

Have you ever felt that? Job did. Job—that great and godly man—felt that way.

Have there been times in your life during which you felt God was against you? Have you ever felt that God was nowhere to be found? Maybe you are in one of those situations right now. Take some time to reflect or remember, and describe the situation two ways: 1) This is how it looked to me; 2) this is how it looked to God. Or 1) This is how it *seemed*; and 2) this is how it truly *was*.

What is the troubling situation you have in mind?

_____

_____

_____

_____

_____

How would you apply your situation to the following two views?

My view:

God's view:

If you can't identify God's view, that's okay. What is important for now is that you recognize He has one—and it may not be the same as yours.

Day Three

2 Corinthians 1:8-9

In yesterday's lesson we examined Job's suffering and began to redefine the experience of suffering for the Christian. We saw that God has a purpose in our suffering, whether we can see it or not. God was sovereign over Job's circumstances at each step along the way.

You might say, "Well, that's the Old Testament. And besides, Job was a unique case." Today we will go to the New Testament to find another example of one who suffered. Look at the apostle Paul. Second Corinthians 1:8-9 records his words:

We do not want you to be unaware, brethren, of our affliction which came to us in Asia, that we were burdened excessively, beyond our strength, so that we despaired even of life; indeed, we had the sentence of death within ourselves so that we would not trust in ourselves, but in God who raises the dead.

The Bible gives several purposes for suffering, but we are focusing on one common purpose for our troubles—to bring us to this place of brokenness. In this passage, we see something that seems to contradict a concept I believed for many years of my life.

I've always heard it said that God will not put any burden on you greater than you can bear. Have you heard that? I grew up being taught that. I want to tell you something: Just because you've heard something said a thousand times in church doesn't mean it's true. The measure of truth is the Bible. What God says is true, regardless of what I may feel or think or have always believed. Do you believe the Bible? Then let's let the Bible be our final authority. I no longer believe that God will not let you have burdens greater than you can bear. I believe that God *will* let you have burdens greater than you can bear. He *intends* for you to have burdens greater than you can bear.

I know some people may say, "Wait a minute. What about 1 Corinthians 10:13?" Read the verse and you will see that it is talking about temptation to sin, and that isn't what I'm talking about right now. That verse is referring to testing that incites us to do evil. "No temptation has seized you except what is common to man" (1 Corinthians 10:13 NIV). I'm not talking about temptation, I'm talking about burdens.

We'll put it in the context of this passage so you can see it in the Word of God. God *will* allow you to be burdened beyond your own abilities.

Use 2 Corinthians 1:8-9 to answer the questions that follow.

> *We do not want you to be unaware, brethren, of our affliction which came to us in Asia, that we were burdened excessively, beyond our strength, so that we despaired even of life; indeed, we had the sentence of death within ourselves so that we would not trust in ourselves, but in God who raises the dead.*

What was Paul doing when this great trouble came into his life? Was he living in sin, or was he obeying the Lord?

_____

_____

What are some words and phrases that Paul uses to describe his problem?

_____

_____

1 Corinthians 10:13

"We had the sentence of death within ourselves so that we would not trust in ourselves, but in God who raises the dead."

2 Corinthians 1:8-9

What does Paul say about his ability to endure the difficulty?

_____

_____

What does Paul say the purpose of his difficulty was?

_____

_____

> *There it is!*
> *In the Bible!*
> *A burden*
> *that is greater*
> *than we can bear.*

Let's walk through these two verses step by step. First of all, Paul tells us his problem seemed to come out of nowhere. "This problem *came to us*." Have you ever felt like that? There you are, walking through life, minding your own business, and here comes trouble! You were ambushed. That was Paul's experience.

Then Paul says his problem was excessive (verse 8). "We were burdened *excessively*." Now, brace yourself. He says this burden was "beyond our strength." The NIV says this burden was "more than our ability to endure it." The burden was more than he could endure. It was beyond his strength. There it is! In the Bible! A burden that is *greater than we can bear*.

Lest there be any confusion about it, he goes on to say, "so that we despaired even of life." Do you know what that means? "We wished we could die!" "But Paul, don't you understand faith?" some may ask him. Yes, he did. Better than many of us. He also understood what it meant to be human and to admit his humanity.

Let's recap how Paul has described his burden. He said

- *it was excessive*

- *it was more than he could bear*

- *it was so heavy, he wished he could die*

Do you see how many times and how many ways he keeps making this point? You and I cannot dispute it.

Why would God allow a man like Paul to experience excessive burdens? Paul was going through life just trying to serve, to be obedient to God's call. Why would God allow a burden greater than Paul could bear? Paul told us why. He told us his troubles served a divine purpose in his life. Why did God allow this burden? For this reason: "In order that we should not trust in ourselves, but in God, who raises the dead." God allowed Paul's intense, excessive, overwhelming burden so Paul would learn not to trust in his own self-sufficiency. The burden was more than he could bear so Paul would be very sure to let Jesus be the one who bore the burden in him and through him.

Consider again the text in Job. Read chapter 23, verse 10: "He knows the way that I take; when he has tested me, I will come forth as gold." Why does God allow burdens in our lives that are more than we can bear? It is so we will come to the end of our self-sufficiency. We hear Christians say sometimes, "The burden is great, but I'm not going to give up." I'm sorry. You're only going to prolong the inevitable. I hear people say, "The burden is tremendous, but I'm not going to let go." I always think, *Don't you know that God will outlast you? You will let go! He'll wait until you do.*

Job 23:10

He will wait until we let go of self-sufficiency, until we let go of our own fleshly techniques for living the Christian life. He wants to bring us to the end of ourselves.

Maybe you're going through troubles right now. One reason for any difficulty is to bring us to that place of brokenness. Your troubles didn't just happen. God has allowed these troubles to come to you. God has good reasons for allowing suffering. One reason is, God uses suffering to expose our flesh patterns. Often we don't know what our functional source of life is until trouble comes. Trouble reveals the functional source of life. In other words, what source of life do we actually operate from? Suffering will show you what you are relying on. Can you see why this is important and how it can be a good thing in your life?

Problems are often God's most effective tools for bringing our self-reliance into the light. Understand, though, that having big problems doesn't mean the same thing as coming to brokenness. It is possible to suffer and not be broken. Don't think that just because you've suffered that you've been broken. Let me repeat, it is possible to suffer and not be broken. Suffering *may* lead to brokenness, but that doesn't have to be the case. Brokenness is when we come to the end of our confidence in the flesh.

As we've learned, *flesh* refers to the techniques a person utilizes to manage his own life when he's not trusting in the sufficiency of Jesus Christ. It is self-reliance. Remember that flesh can look either good or bad.

One example is found in Luke 15:11-32. In this parable are two stories: the story of the prodigal son and the story of the elder brother.

> *A man had two sons. The younger of them said to his father, "Father, give me the share of the estate that falls to me." So he divided his wealth between them. And not many days later, the younger son gathered everything together and went on a journey into a distant country, and there he squandered his estate with loose living. Now when he had spent everything, a severe famine occurred in that country, and he began to be impoverished. So he went and hired himself out to one of the citizens of that country, and he sent him into his fields to feed swine. And he would have gladly filled his stomach with the pods that the swine were eating, and no one was giving anything to him. But when he came to his senses, he said, "How many of my father's hired men have more than enough bread, but I am dying here with hunger! I will get up and go to my father, and will say to him, 'Father, I have sinned against heaven, and in your sight;*

Day Four

Luke 15:11-32

Luke 15:11-32

I am no longer worthy to be called your son; make me as one of your hired men.'" So he got up and came to his father. But while he was still a long way off, his father saw him and felt compassion for him, and ran and embraced him and kissed him. And the son said to him, "Father, I have sinned against heaven and in your sight; I am no longer worthy to be called your son." But the father said to his slaves, "Quickly bring out the best robe and put it on him, and put a ring on his hand and sandals on his feet; and bring the fattened calf, kill it, and let us eat and celebrate; for this son of mine was dead and has come to life again; he was lost and has been found." And they began to celebrate.

Now his older son was in the field, and when he came and approached the house, he heard music and dancing. And he summoned one of the servants and began inquiring what these things could be. And he said to him, "Your brother has come, and your father has killed the fattened calf because he has received him back safe and sound." But he became angry and was not willing to go in; and his father came out and began pleading with him. But he answered and said to his father, "Look! For so many years I have been serving you and I have never neglected a command of yours; and yet you have never given me a young goat, so that I might celebrate with my friends; but when this son of yours came, who has devoured your wealth with prostitutes, you killed the fattened calf for him." And he said to him, "Son, you have always been with me, and all that is mine is yours. But we had to celebrate and rejoice, for this brother of yours was dead and has begun to live, and was lost and has been found."

When the prodigal son left the Father, was his behavior good or was his behavior bad? It was _____.

When the prodigal son recognized his condition, did he say he was no longer his father's son? What did he say instead?

_____

_____

Why did the prodigal believe he was not worthy to be called a son or treated as a son?

_____

_____

Look at the older brother, the pious son. While the prodigal son was off in the distant land, was the older son's behavior good or was his behavior bad? _____

On what basis did he assume his father should be pleased with him?

_____

_____

Let's examine these two sons. The prodigal son went off to get his needs met apart from his father. He asked for his inheritance, left home, and apparently spent all his money on a hedonistic lifestyle. Finally, he came to the end of himself. He was miserable. He foolishly sinned. He lived out of his flesh. He was miserable.

The elder brother stayed home. I call him "the pious son." While the prodigal was in the far country wasting his money on wicked living, the proud, pious son stayed home and continued to work on the farm and go to church with his dad every Sunday and act responsibly.

Do you remember when the prodigal son came home? He prepared a speech he was going to give to his father. He was going to say to his father, "I've sinned against heaven and against you, and I'm no longer worthy to be called your son. Make me as one of your hired men." In verse 21 we read, "And the son said to him, 'Father, I have sinned against heaven and in your sight; I am no longer worthy to be called your son.' But the father said…" The father interrupted him. He never let the boy finish his speech.

Luke 15:21

> *This is a story about the Father's acceptance.*

I used to think the story of the prodigal son was a story about God's forgiveness. I thought it taught us that if we'd just come on home and ask for forgiveness, God would forgive us. That's not what it's about. That boy was already forgiven. He didn't even have to ask.

This is a story about the Father's acceptance. The rebellious son thought he had to come home and be a servant. Oh, how many times I've been there. I would have been out in the far country and, in my mind, in my imagination (which did not align itself with Scripture), I would see myself coming back to God and saying, "Oh, God, if You'll just forgive me this time, I'll serve You better." And it's as if the Father said, "Son, don't you get it? It's not about service. The bottom line is this—*you are My son!* I accept you, whether you are in the far country, or here, or wherever you are."

The prodigal comes home and the father immediately says, "Let's have a party!" So the music starts and they fire up the barbeque.

There's music and dancing in the house. The father starts looking around for the older brother and he's not there. So the father asks, "Where's my older son?" Somebody answers, "He's outside." So the father goes to find him. He asks the older son why he won't come in, and the son says, "I've served you faithfully and I've never sinned against you. But you've never given me a party."

This older brother, the pious son, made the same mistake as his prodigal brother! They both thought their acceptance by the father depended on how well they performed. The younger brother thought he should be rejected because he didn't perform well. The older brother thought he should be accepted because he had performed well. The father said to the older son, "Son, all that I have is yours." In other words, "Don't you know who you are?"

> *The father said to the older son, "Son, all that I have is yours."*

The younger brother was miserable after he had miserably sinned. The older brother was miserable after he had faithfully served. We might say he had demonstrated negative flesh patterns, but the older brother demonstrated positive flesh patterns. But whether independent living looks positive or negative, they both have one thing in common. They are both flesh.

With which son do you identify most? "I identify most with the _____ son." Do you look at your failures and feel that God could never accept you? Or do you look at your rule-following performance and feel that God accepts you as long as you do the right thing?

_____

_____

Would you surrender your self-reliance to God right now and take some time to let the truth of grace fill you and set you free? Write out your thoughts.

God uses problems to bring us to brokenness. He wants to deliver you from the tree of the knowledge of good and evil. He wants to get you off the good branch as much as He wants to get you off the evil branch. He wants to get you into the place where you abide in Jesus Christ and let Him live His life through you.

Your flesh patterns may look good. You may be a good churchgoing person, and you may do all the right things but still be living out of your flesh. Suffering can reveal that. Suffering can become the catalyst for brokenness. Remember the meaning of brokenness? It is a condition that exists when a person has given up all confidence in his own ability to manage life. That's where God wants you. The place of brokenness, where you give up on your life and begin to experience His life—that's where God is bringing you.

1 Corinthians 1:27-30

Read 1 Corinthians 1:27-30. The Bible teaches there that you don't get strong enough, you get weak enough. Maybe you've been praying the wrong prayer. Maybe you've been praying, "Lord, make me stronger," when what you need to be praying is, "Lord, make me weaker." Our weakness is the doorway to His strength. Problems can be the bridge that brings us to the place of weakness, causing our problems to be one of the best things that could happen to us.

I began to serve local churches as a pastor when I was 19 years old and continued in that role for 21 years. I served numerous churches and, through the years, for the most part, I felt successful as a pastor. The churches I served grew, and little by little I began to gain a sense of significance through what I did.

Before I moved to Atlanta, Georgia, I served an Alabama church that seemed like paradise on earth. It was a wonderful place for a pastor to be. The congregation dearly loved and constantly affirmed me. The church was growing, and in fact had been recognized as the fastest-growing church in our area for a number of years. Wonderful things were happening. I never planned to leave there.

I began to pray, "Lord, I want to know You more intimately than I've ever known You before. I want to experience all that I can of You. Lord, I want to know the depths of who You are." One day I received a call from a man in Atlanta, who introduced himself as the chairman of a committee that was searching for a pastor for their church. He asked if his committee could come over and meet with me. In this conversation, I sensed from the Holy Spirit that I should let them come, and they did.

After some time it became apparent that God was leading me to leave my church in Alabama and to move to Atlanta, Georgia, to become their pastor. Their church had been declining in every measurable way for five years, but I knew God was leading me there. I certainly believed that when I got there, things would turn around.

When the Sunday came that I stood before my congregation in Alabama to tell them I was leaving, people began to cry. I did too. I didn't want to go, but I knew God was calling me.

Driving away from that town toward Atlanta was a difficult and emotional journey. As we approached Atlanta, I thought, *If God is leading me from such a wonderful place to take me to Atlanta, I can only imagine what will happen—how large the church will grow, how successful I'll be.*

I moved into that church and began to work with all my strength. For the first several months, I put in many long hours. But after a few months, what was going on in that church surprised me. *Nothing* was going on. It was the first time I'd ever experienced anything like that. Always before when I'd gone to a new church, immediately it had begun to grow and things began to happen. But this time, nothing was happening. I felt some discouragement, but I stepped back and took a look and reevaluated the situation. I determined I was going to go forward with renewed commitment and greater zeal. Time passed. Nothing happened. My discouragement spiraled down into depression. I did everything I knew how to do to cause the church to grow. In spite of everything, the church continued to hold, and even decline.

At the end of my first year in that church, I was preparing to give a State of the Church address. Usually, in my State of the Church address, I told about all the good things that had gone on in the church. As I looked at the statistics, which was the only way I measured success back then, I concluded we were in a sorry state. I didn't have the courage to tell them the truth and I didn't have the strength to pretend. It was October 6, 1990, when I was on my face in my office. It was two o'clock in the morning and I was crying. I was crying like grown men don't often cry. The kind of crying that leaves you breathless. I didn't understand. I had moved from discouragement to depression, and now I was at a place of absolute despair. It made no sense to me.

I was lying on my face and I said, "God, I don't understand this. I don't understand why You brought me here. Did You bring me here so the church would die? Where I was, the church was growing and I felt loved. Here the church is declining and I don't feel accepted by the people. Why did You bring me here?" I felt anger rise up in me. Lying on my face, I lifted up my head and looked toward the heavens and I cried out a question that was really an accusation: "God, I've been serving You since I was 16 years old. I've given my whole life to You. What do You want from me?" It was a rhetorical question. I didn't expect an answer. But the Lord did answer. "Steve, I just want you." I didn't expect that answer. I thought He wanted me for what I could do for Him. I thought He wanted me and called and chose me so I could build big churches. Instead, I came to understand He just wanted me.

> *I thought He wanted me and called me and chose me so I could build big churches.*
>
> *Instead, I came to understand that He just wanted me.*

My mind turned to a piece of paper a guest speaker had given me a few weeks before. I had laid that piece of paper on my computer table by my desk. I was lying on the floor, but I reached up and pulled that piece of paper down and began to read it. Across the top it had the words *Absolute Surrender.* It had a list of things this speaker had suggested we all surrender to God. Rights we should give up. Things like dreams and hopes, past successes and failures, relationships, expectations. It had a list of rights we should surrender to the Lord, things like the right to pleasant circumstances, the right to be accepted, the right to see results, the right to be loved, the right to be used by God.

I began to pray my way down that list. I began to systematically empty myself of the things that had given me a sense of value as a person. When I reached the end of that list, I was like a blank piece of paper. I gave up everything I'd been holding onto. I was emptied. Absolute surrender. I signed my name at the bottom of that paper beneath a paragraph that said,

> *"I give God permission to do anything He wants to do with me, in me, toward me, or through me that would glorify Him. I once claimed these rights as mine, but now they belong to God and are under His control, and He can do whatever He pleases."*

I signed that paper and dated it. Now, *I* was a blank piece of paper.

That night was a turning point in my life. It was the doorway through which I had to pass. Brokenness. Remember that brokenness is a condition that exists when we have given up all confidence in our own ability to manage life. It's not an event. I'm not saying you have to have an event like I did. It is a condition, but sometimes the condition is initiated by an event.

I came to the place of brokenness that night. I took my hands off my own life and said, "Lord Jesus, my life is Yours." A few weeks later, the Lord began to give me the revelation of my identity in Christ. But I could never have received that revelation, that understanding, had I not come to the place of brokenness.

What are the problems in your life now? There may be a good reason for it. Stop praying for God to help you and instead cooperate with the Holy Spirit. He may be working to bring you to brokenness. The results of brokenness in our lives can be seen when we give up on managing our own lives.

Brokenness means we become teachable. Then we become hungry for Him more than anything else. Have you come to this place of brokenness in your life? The issue isn't whether you have suffered. You may have suffered and not have come to brokenness. Have you come to the place of brokenness? God may be using your troubles today to bring you to that very place.

> *Brokenness is a doorway through which you must pass if you want to enter into the fullness of your identity in Christ.*

Your heavenly Father loves you too much to rescue you from your circumstances. He didn't rescue Jesus from the cross. What makes you think He should rescue you from your problem? He wants you to come to the end of confidence in yourself so that you come to the place of absolute surrender and are ready to pray this kind of prayer: "Father, I acknowledge Your right to do anything You want to do to me, with me, or through me that would glorify You. I once claimed these rights as mine, but now they belong to You and are under Your control. You can do anything with them that You please."

Brokenness is a doorway through which you must pass if you want to enter into the fullness of your identity in Christ. Are you willing to walk through that door? Can you see how your problems may be the best thing that could have happened to you? They may be used by God to bring you to the end of yourself.

Brokenness is pictured by Isaac on the altar, his father holding the knife. Isaac could have struggled and resisted, but he surrendered voluntarily to his father's hand. As Isaac lay on the altar, it was up to his father what would happen next. That's what it means to be a living sacrifice.

Romans 12:1

> *I urge you, brethren, by the mercies of God, to present your bodies a living and holy sacrifice, acceptable to God, which is your spiritual service of worship" (Romans 12:1).*

Are you willing to come to that place of total abandonment to Jesus?

What do you need to let go of in order to come to a place of absolute surrender? Will you empty yourself of the things that have given you a sense of value as a person and become a blank piece of paper? Write out the things the Holy Spirit brings to your mind.

_____

_____

_____

_____

_____

_____

_____

_____

_____

If you sense God speaking to you, sign the following statement:

I give God permission to do anything He wants to do with me, in me, toward me, or through me that would glorify Him. I once claimed these rights as mine, but now they belong to God and are under His control, and He can do whatever He pleases.

Signed,

Problems can be used by the Holy Spirit to bring you to brokenness. Brokenness opens the door for you to enter into the experience of the living Christ expressing His life through you. There is no other entry into the supernatural reality of the grace walk. You may not feel like it now, but your problems can be the best thing that could ever have happened to you.

You Must Know Who You Are to Change What You Do

Day One

In the last two weeks, you've learned two truths that are vital to experiencing the grace walk. You have seen that trying to improve your behavior won't do it—rather, it is nothing more than a flesh trip. You've learned that God's solution for our insistence on self-improvement begins with *brokenness*—a condition in which a person has given up all confidence in his ability to manage his own life. God wants to bring you to the place of brokenness and absolute surrender so He can usher you into the experience of Christ as your life.

Many Christians think they can become all they should be by changing the things they do. In reality, the opposite is true. It is when we understand *who we are* that our behavior changes. *Doing flows from being—not vice versa.*

2 Corinthians 5:17

In this week's lesson we will move into the heart of the message of our identity in Christ. The Bible says in 2 Corinthians 5:17 that at the moment of your salvation, you became a new creation. "If anyone is in Christ, he is a new creature; the old things passed away; behold, new things have come." You have become a brand-new person. In order to begin a study of this fact, I want us to start this week by examining the nature of man.

It is important to understand how God has created us. The Bible teaches that man is created in the image of God. God is a triune being, existing in three Persons. God has made man a triune being consisting of spirit, soul, and body. In 1 Thessalonians 5:23, for example, the Scripture teaches the threefold nature of man.

1 Thessalonians 5:23

Read the following Scripture passage and answer the questions that follow.

May the God of peace Himself sanctify you entirely; and may your spirit and soul and body be preserved complete, without blame at the coming of our Lord Jesus Christ. Faithful is He who calls you, and He also will bring it to pass (1 Thessalonians 5:23-24).

1 Thessalonians 5:23-24

What does the word *sanctify* mean?

_____

_____

Who will do the sanctifying?

_____

_____

How complete will the work of sanctifying be? What is the word that describes the extent of the work?

_____

_____

Name the three parts of your being that will be "preserved complete, without blame."

_____

_____

Who will "bring it to pass"? In other words, who will accomplish that which God desires of you?

_____

Do you see that these very important statements about God, who works in you to accomplish His will for you, set out in no uncertain terms the three aspects of man? Paul clearly differentiates between spirit, soul, and body.

We Live in a Body

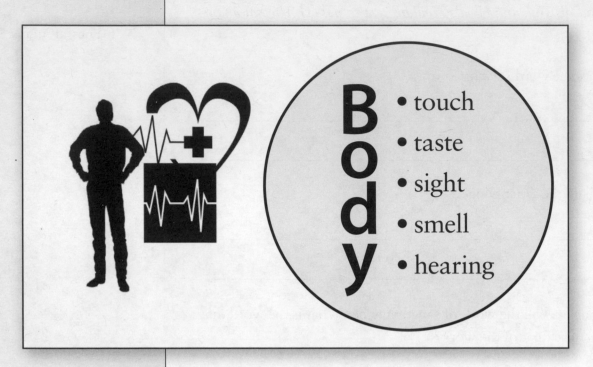

Your body is not who you are. It is only where you live.

Let's start looking at man by considering the outermost part, the body. The body is where we live. Sometimes the New Testament calls the body a house. It is the place where the real "you" lives. Through your body, you relate to the world around you by means of your five senses. Your body is not who you are. It is only where you live. Like every house, it gets progressively older. Your body is going to eventually wear out. It's going to collapse like all houses do because that's what happens with age.

Years ago I read a *Reader's Digest* article that quoted an 88-year-old woman, who described it like this:

You see me as an ancient old woman. But I want to tell you something. This is me inside here. I haven't changed. I'm just stuck within this broken old body and I can't get out. It hurts me, and it won't move right, and it gets tired whenever I try to do anything. But the real me is not what you see. I am a prisoner within this decaying body.

This lady understood that the body is not who we are. It's only where we live. Mankind lives in a body.

We Possess a Soul

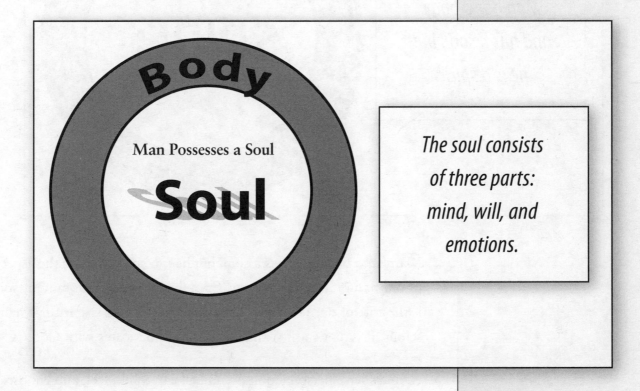

Man Possesses a Soul

Soul

The soul consists of three parts: mind, will, and emotions.

Not only do we have a body, but the Bible tells us that man also possesses a soul. While the body is sense-conscious, relating to the world around us, the soul is self-conscious and socially conscious. The soul consists of three parts: mind, will, and emotions. Through his soul, man thinks and reasons; he decides and chooses, and he feels. Another word for *soul* is the word *personality*. Man is not a soul; he possesses a soul, but he is not a soul.

Man Is a Spirit

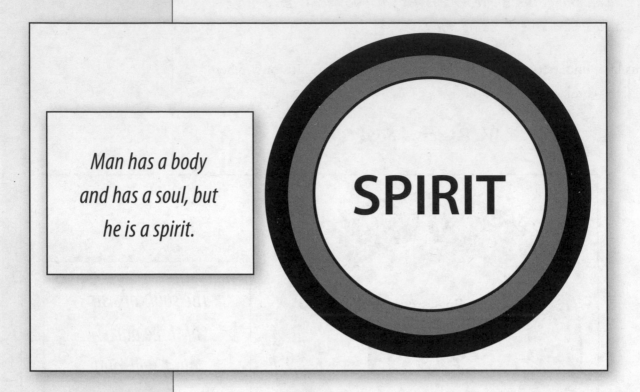

> *Man has a body and has a soul, but he is a spirit.*
>
> **SPIRIT**

Man *has* a body and *has* a soul, but he *is* a spirit. This is the aspect of our nature that sets us apart from the animal kingdom. Our spirit is the core of our being. Man *is* a spirit. The spirit is spiritually conscious. It is that spirit within us that communicates with God.

Animals have personalities. An animal can think, feel, and choose. So, in that sense, we might say that an animal has a soul, but it doesn't have a spirit. That is where you and I are different from animals.

For many years, our family had a little puppy at home, and I could see her soul functioning at times. When she had done wrong, her personality became evident. If I came into the house and she had done wrong—and it was usually the same "wrong thing" every time we left the house—I could see her soul (personality) move into action. I could see she had feelings as she crouched down low like she was afraid. I saw her mind at work as she looked around to find my wife to run to and be rescued. Or else she tried to find a couch or bed she could hide under. I saw her will because she made her choice and darted for either my wife or a hiding place. I saw her personality in action. My little puppy had a soul, but she didn't have a spirit. Nobody would ever have called her a "Christian" dog.

The spirit is what distinguishes humans from animals. It is the spirit that communicates with God. You are a spirit. Someone has said that man is a spirit who has a soul and lives in a body. The spirit is the core of your identity. Whatever you are in the spirit is who you are.

What are the three aspects of man's nature and what is the function of each?

1. _____

_____

2. _____

_____

3. _____

_____

As you conclude your study today, pause and reflect on how you have been created in the image of God. No other living creature apart from man has known that privilege. Pause right now and thank Him for creating you in His image.

We have seen that man's nature is such that he is a three-part being. Let's now consider the identity of Christians. Remember when Adam and Eve sinned in the garden? They stepped away from God and established an identity separate from Him. Since that time the curse of man apart from God is that he senses the need to establish an identity for himself.

Accomplishments

There are various ways people try to establish a meaningful identity in this world. One way is by *accomplishments*. The world focuses on doing, but God focuses on being. Performance is the world's way to establish identity. When we don't know our identity in Christ, we may fall into the trap of trying to find identity through the things we do.

Performance-based acceptance is the wrong way to establish an identity. With man, what we do determines who we are, but with God, knowing who we are will determine what we do. Do you see the difference between the two?

What are some of the accomplishments in your life that you may have looked to in order to define who you are as a human being?

_____

_____

_____

_____

_____

Relationships

Another way identity may be established is by relationships. I'll give you an example: marriage. In marriage, the bride is joined to the groom. When Melanie married me, she took my name. Her last name changed to McVey. She took my identity. She gave up her old identity and ours merged into one. We came together in what the Bible describes as two becoming one flesh.

Another example is birth. Melanie and I have four children. My children have my identity. My life is in them. That will always be the case. They have my identity because they were born to us. Their identity had nothing to do with what they would do or not do. It is the result of their birth.

God has established our identity through Christ. You and I have been joined together with Jesus Christ through marriage. We've also been joined to Him by birth. Consequently, we now have a new identity. Do you know what our identity is? Let's examine what the Scripture says about who you are.

In the following Scriptures, underline any words or phrases that describe who you are.

...To the church of God which is at Corinth, to those who have been sanctified in Christ Jesus, saints by calling, with all who in every place call on the name of our Lord Jesus Christ, their Lord and ours (1 Corinthians 1:2).

1 Corinthians 1:2

We are His workmanship, created in Christ Jesus for good works, which God prepared beforehand so that we would walk in them (Ephesians 2:10).

Ephesians 2:10

If, by the trespass of the one man, death reigned through that one man, how much more will those who receive God's abundant provision of grace and of the gift of righteousness reign in life through the one man, Jesus Christ (Romans 5:17).

Romans 5:17

…To the praise of the glory of His grace, which He freely bestowed on us in the Beloved (Ephesians 1:6).

Ephesians 1:6

Who Are You?

1. A saint. In 1 Corinthians 1:2, Paul addresses the people of the church at Corinth as saints. He certainly had to be talking about an identity that stemmed from their spiritual birth, because their behavior wasn't saintly by any means. He calls them saints in chapter 1 and then spends the rest of his letter telling them to start living like the saints they are. Don't be uncomfortable with being called a saint, because that's what God calls you! The New Testament refers to Christians as saints 62 times. That doesn't mean you live a sinless life, but that God has set you apart and placed the life of Christ within you.

1 Corinthians 1:2

> *Don't be uncomfortable with being called a saint, because that's what God calls you!*

2. A work of art. You are God's work of art. Ephesians 2:10 calls you "God's workmanship." The word *workmanship* is the Greek word *poema,* from which we get the English word *poem.* You are God's heavenly piece of poetry on earth.

Ephesians 2:10

3. Righteous and holy. You are righteous and holy. In Romans 5:17 Paul says you have received "the gift of righteousness." The Lord Jesus is your righteousness. When you received Him, your spirit was filled with His righteousness. What you are at the spirit level determines your real identity. When you do not behave righteously, you are being inconsistent with who you are. First Corinthians 3:1-17 says you are the temple of God and are holy.

Romans 5:17

1 Corinthians 3:1-17

4. Accepted. You are fully accepted by God. You are accepted because you are in Christ (read Ephesians 1:6). Because Christ has received you and He is fully accepted by the Father, you are fully accepted as well. You don't need to change a single thing about yourself for God to accept you. Your acceptance isn't based on what you do, but on who you are.

Ephesians 1:6

Read the following verses about your identity and fill in the blanks:

2 Corinthians 5:21

2 Corinthians 5:21: "He made Him who knew no _Sin_ to be

Sin for us on our behalf, so that we might become the

Righteousness of God in Him."

What does God's Word call you in that verse?

_____

_____

1 Corinthians 3:17

1 Corinthians 3:17: "The temple of God is holy and that is

_____."

What is a temple?

_____

_____

Whose temple are you?

_____

_____

Because the Holy Spirit of the Holy God resides in you—makes you His home—what does that say about you?

_____

_____

_____

_____

If you go to many churches next week and ask the people, "Are you holy?" most will answer, "I'm trying to be." Our response to such a statement should be, "Stop trying. Start trusting. Believe what God says about you. Just be who you are." Pause now and thank your Father for the new identity He has given you in Christ Jesus!

In Ephesians 4:24, the apostle Paul wrote, "Put on the new self, which in the likeness of God has been created in righteousness and holiness of the truth." God has already made you righteous and holy. Past tense. It's done. Now, the Bible says, put on the new self—act like who you are.

God's description of the Christian is that we're saints, we're righteous, we're a divine work of art, we're holy, we're one with Christ. Let me say it again—*one with Him*. Jesus is not *in* your life—He *is* your life!

First Corinthians 6:17 is great news: "The one who joins himself to the Lord is one spirit with Him." Why is that such good news? It's because Jesus is not just in your life. It's better than that. He *is* your life. You have become one with Him.

You have a new nature. Second Peter 1:4 states, "He has granted to us His precious and magnificent promises, so that by them you may become partakers of the divine nature." You have the divine nature—the nature of Jesus. Jesus Christ has given you His very nature. Before, sin filled your spirit, so your identity was that of a sinner. Now, Christ dwells in your spirit, so your identity is that of a Christian. If Christ is your life, if He has given you His nature, then you've taken on His characteristics. His holiness, His righteousness. You are one with Him.

Imagine that I had an egg and I told you I had taken this egg from an incubator. Let's let that egg represent a human being. The shell represents the body. The white represents the soul. The yolk represents the spirit. While it isn't biologically accurate, let's imagine that the life or essence of the chicken is the yolk.

Ephesians 4:24

1 Corinthians 6:17

2 Peter 1:4

What if I said to you, "This incubating egg is going to produce a defective, deformed chick because there's something wrong with the yolk." Then imagine if I took that egg and inserted a needle through the shell, through the white, and into the yolk and extracted that bad yolk. In its place I inject a healthy, fresh yolk where the old yolk had been, and I put it back into the incubator so it continues to incubate until it hatches a perfectly healthy chick. How would you answer this question: Is that chicken a changed chicken? No, it's not. It is an *exchanged* chicken.

> *God didn't just change your life. It's better than that. He exchanged your life.*

I've got good news for you—you're not the same bird you were before salvation! God didn't just *change* your life. It's better than that. He *exchanged* your life. He has taken out the old you, the sinner, and Jesus has come to take His place in you. You are one with Christ. You have the nature of Jesus Christ. Do you believe that? I hope you do, because the Bible says so. You're now an expression of divine life.

Colossians 3:4

Colossians 3:4 says, "When Christ, *who is our life,* is revealed, then you also will be revealed with Him in glory." We are not only containers, but conduits of divine life. Jesus will both live in us and will flow through us. He is all of Himself *in you*. He is who He is *in you*. If you have Jesus, you have everything He is and everything He possesses.

What do you feel is missing in your life? What do you need? Be very specific.

_____

_____

_____

Do you believe that you have Jesus in you?

_____

Do you believe that you have *all* of Jesus living in you?

_____

Is there anything Jesus does not possess?

_____

Ask God for a revelation of everything that is already yours. Receive it with thanksgiving.

Common Misunderstandings

There are some common misunderstandings about this concept, the righteousness of the believer. Those who fail to understand that righteousness is *received* often falsely believe it can be *achieved* through various means. I want you to recognize several misunderstandings about righteousness. We will consider the first misunderstanding in today's study and continue with others tomorrow.

If you think you can become righteous by your own efforts, I need to warn you that self-effort produces only one kind of righteousness—*self*-righteousness. The righteousness that is from God comes by faith, and it is a gift to us in the person of Jesus Christ. Self-righteousness will prevent us from ever experiencing the grace walk.

Righteousness by progression. Some people believe we become more and more righteous as we walk with the Lord. But it's not by what you do that you become righteous. The Scripture says in 1 Corinthians 1:30 that Jesus is your righteousness:

1 Corinthians 1:30

By His doing you are in Christ Jesus, who became to us wisdom from God, and righteousness and sanctification, and redemption, so that, just as it is written, "Let him who boasts boast in the Lord."

So I ask you—how righteous are you? Look at it this way: On a scale of 1 to 100, how righteous is Jesus Christ? 100. On the chart below, shade in the bar representing Jesus to the 100 level.

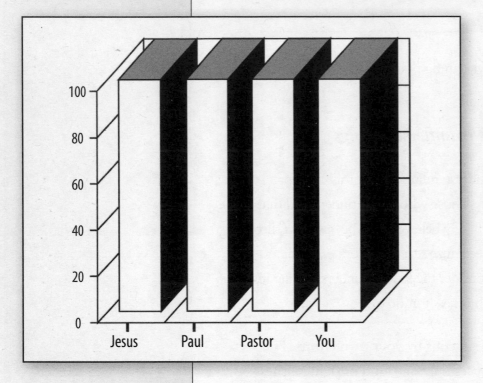

Now, using that same scale, shade in the percentage of righteousness possessed by the apostle Paul, then the one representing your pastor. Finally, look at yourself. How righteous would you say you are? Shade the bar representing you.

Now, what percentage did you give to each of those listed? Every bar should be shaded in to 100, including you. You are as righteous as Jesus Christ because Jesus Christ *is* our righteousness. We may not always *act* righteous, but that fact doesn't change the reality of who we are. Don't allow your feelings to dictate what you believe about this matter. Let God's Word have the final say about it. That is the ultimate authority for Christians, right?

Let me illustrate the point this way: Imagine if I found a ring at church. I brought the ring in and showed it to everybody and asked whose it was, but no one claimed it. Someone might say, "You found the ring. No one has claimed it, so it's yours to keep." I look at the ring, and it looks like its stone is about a one-carat diamond. Immediately I think, *I wonder what that's worth.*

So I take it to a friend and ask him what he thinks the diamond is worth. He tells me it's worth about six or seven thousand dollars. Then I take it to another friend and he says, "No, that's not a real diamond. That is cubic zirconium. I think it is only worth about three hundred dollars." I then take it to yet another friend who looks at it and says, "That came out of a toy machine. That's just plastic. Why, it's not worth more than three dollars."

At this point I have opinions that range from three dollars to seven thousand dollars. How do I know the value of the ring? I take the ring to an appraiser, and he sets a value on it based on the price someone would be willing to pay for it. So if someone were willing to pay five thousand dollars for the ring, then the value of the ring would be five thousand dollars. I could look at the ring and say, "This ring *equals* five thousand dollars." The ring and the five thousand dollars have the same value.

> *Unless you know your identity in Christ, you are always asking in one way or another, "What is my value? What am I worth?"*

When you and I came into the world, we were born with a big question mark over our heads. The question was, "What is my value? What am I worth?" Unless you know your identity in Christ, you are always asking in one way or another, "What is my value? What am I worth?" We try to establish in our own minds what our value is based on what other people tell us. (We will probably get varying appraisals, depending on whether we ask our mother or our employer.)

But there is a way you can know your value. Bring yourself before the expert. Come to God and say, "Can you tell me my value?" God will answer, "Yes, I can." He will determine your value in the same way the appraiser determines the value of the ring. It hinges on the price someone is willing to pay for you.

God could say, "You have been bought with a price. And I am the One who bought you. What I paid for you is Jesus." Isn't that response biblical? Then would it be accurate to say that to God, you are of equal value to Jesus? It almost sounds blasphemous, doesn't it? But I want to assure you that your heavenly Father treasures you like He treasures His own Son because Christ is your life. You are now one with Him. You are 100 percent righteous because *He* is 100 percent righteous.

In fact, you will be no more righteous in heaven than you are right now. I'm not talking about your behavior. I'm talking about your nature. I'm talking about *who you are*. Righteousness by progression is a lie. Do you believe what the Bible says—that you are righteous by nature? Write your answer, yes or no.

_____

Write out an affirmative statement of your belief. Write in your own hand: I AM RIGHTEOUS.

I AM RIGHTEOUS

_____

_____

Read Romans 5:17 and complete the following sentence:

The righteousness that I now possess came to me as a

_____

through the abundance of God's

_____ .

The life-changing truth we are studying this week that will cause you to be able to experience the grace walk is that we must know who we are to change what we do. When you know you are righteous in Jesus Christ, that knowledge will become the catalyst for a transformation in your lifestyle.

Today, we are going to continue with a look at misunderstandings about the truth that we have been given the righteousness of Jesus Christ. This is a vital aspect of experiencing the grace walk. If you aren't persuaded by the Holy Spirit of your righteousness in Christ, you won't be able to move forward.

Righteousness by position. This is a common misconception about the Christian's righteousness. It is a teaching that suggests Christians are righteous only in a theoretical sort of way, based on our position in Christ. A person who holds this view would argue, "I'm not really righteous. It's just positional. It's just the way God sees me. He only *sees* me as righteous."

To the argument that God only *sees* Christians as righteous, I would state the obvious—however God sees something, that's how it is! God doesn't have opinions that are not grounded in truth. He doesn't have fanciful thoughts based on what he wishes were true. God's thoughts are truth. He sees you as righteous because you *are* righteous. God sees things as they are.

The idea of positional righteousness is a doctrinal hiding place for us when we can't reconcile what the Bible teaches with our experience. We have to try to find some way to explain it. Romans 5:19 says,

Romans 5:19

> As through the one man's disobedience the many were made sinners, even so through the obedience of the One the many will be made righteous.

There is a scholastic field concerning how to study the Bible. Pastors often study it in seminary. It is called *hermeneutics*. In hermeneutics, there are certain principles to which one must adhere when studying the Bible in order to be honest. One of those principles is the principle of consistency. When you interpret the Bible, you must be consistent in your interpretation. Apply the principle of consistency to Romans 5:19.

Romans 5:19

> *As through the one man's disobedience the many were made sinners, even so through the obedience of the One the many will be made righteous (Romans 5:19).*

Are all men sinners literally, or positionally?

_____

Do all men really have a sin nature that causes them to sin?

_____

Then, to be consistent in interpretation, will many be made truly and authentically righteous through Christ?

_____

Either we weren't literally sinners when we were in Adam or else we have literally been made righteous by being in Christ. It's not intellectually honest to divide Romans 5:19 in half and interpret each half in opposite ways.

Righteousness by confession. Another misconception about righteousness is that we maintain it by confession. Some believe you are only righteous if you are "confessed up"—if every infraction has been meticulously confessed and you have asked for forgiveness for everything you have done wrong.

However, it is not by constantly asking God to forgive your sins that you maintain your righteousness. You don't move in and out of righteousness. That which maintains our righteousness is the grace of God. It's not up to you to keep yourself righteous. It's up to Him to keep you righteous. We didn't enter into righteousness by our doing, nor do we maintain righteousness by our doing. We enter into righteousness by His grace and we maintain it by His grace.

What if you left your home tomorrow morning—you had confessed all your sins and asked forgiveness, so you were righteous when you left the house. But on the way to work, someone cut you off in traffic and you thought, or even said, something unkind. Before you had time to repent and confess and ask forgiveness, a truck slammed into you and killed you. Would you go to hell? After all, you had not had time to confess your sin. To hold to such a viewpoint about our righteousness would be a miserable way to live!

Do you know what will happen if you live with the sense that you must continually be confessing your sins in order to be in right standing with God? You will never get to enjoy Jesus. You'll be so busy staring at yourself, you'll never have the chance to glance at Him, let alone gaze at Him. Righteousness by confession is an error.

If you believe you must constantly keep a clean slate through your own confession in order to maintain your righteousness, I want to challenge your thinking. Consider this verse: James 4:17.

James 4:17

> To *him who knows the right thing to do, and does not do it, to him it is sin.*

Is it the right thing to witness about Jesus to everybody we know?

Did you witness to *anybody* about Jesus today?

_____

Is it the right thing to memorize Scripture?

_____

Have you done that this week?

_____

Is it the right thing to pray without ceasing?

_____

How much time have you spent praying today?

_____

If you have failed in the above areas, have you confessed it yet?

_____

If not, according to the idea that we must confess to remain righteous, where does that leave you right now?

_____

I hope you understand my point. I'm not trying to make you feel guilty with the questions above. I want you to recognize it if you hold the erroneous paradigm about confession being necessary to maintain righteousness. It isn't confession that keeps us righteous, it's Jesus. Do we acknowledge it when we sin? Of course we do! That's our nature. We certainly wouldn't try to conceal the fact we've sinned. But it is important to understand that you never lose your righteousness once you are a Christian.

Righteousness by association. There are those who say, "No it's not me who is righteous, it's only Jesus in me." This viewpoint is like finding a diamond in a garbage can. It suggests that we are the garbage can and Jesus is the diamond inside.

I hope you've understood the good news by now. Jesus has transformed you from a garbage can into a work of art. You have been made righteous by a miracle from God. You have been made holy. You have been sanctified. You have become a saint. Not because you did anything to deserve it, but because you just believed what God said and received the life of Jesus.

You're not just a sinner saved by grace. You are much more than that! You are a saint—who sometimes sins. It is not your nature to sin anymore. God has given you the nature of Jesus Christ. You don't have to struggle to be righteous. Righteousness is not achieved by performance, but it is received in the person of Jesus Christ.

Like me, you don't feel righteous all the time. We don't act righteous all the time. But you have a choice to make—what are you going to believe? God's Word or your feelings? God's Word can be trusted. Choose to believe the Word of God.

If you are going to *experience* the grace walk (as opposed to simply adding this teaching to a mental folder labeled "Interesting Truths"), it is necessary to appropriate by faith the truths we have examined this week. Only by knowing who we are will we be empowered to change what we do.

Nobody consistently behaves in a way that is a contradiction of how he perceives himself to be. In other words, what you think about yourself will be the ultimate factor in determining the actions of your lifestyle. That's why we must know who God says we are and believe it by faith, whether we feel it or not.

Review the concepts we studied this week to prepare yourself to go on in the study of the grace walk. Pray that the Holy Spirit will *reveal* the truth to you concerning who you are in Christ, because this is the foundation upon which all the rest of the truths in this book stand.

What are the three aspects of man, and which level is the core and essence of his nature?

Because Jesus lives His life in your spirit, through your soul, and through your body, what are some words that describe who you are?

What are some misconceptions about how righteousness is attained?

What is the truth about how righteousness is attained?

It is my prayer that you are growing in an understanding of your identity in Christ. This issue is the foundation upon which everything necessary to experience the grace walk stands. Without a grasp of our true identity, we will forever be doomed to a never-ending attempt to make ourselves better by trying to change our behavior.

As you conclude this week's study, I want you to simply review the lessons from the past four days. Consider the following topics and respond to the questions concerning each one.

The Nature of Man

What are the three parts of a human being and what is the role of each?

1. _____

2. _____

3. _____

The Believer's True Identity

What are the two ways that people try to establish a meaningful identity in this world?

1. _____

2. _____

In what ways have you seen yourself try to build an identity with the two ways you have identified?

_____

_____

_____

_____

_____

Who are you? Use Bible verses to prove your answers.

1. _____

2. _____

3. _____

4. _____

Misunderstandings About Righteousness

Several misunderstandings about how righteousness is attained were discussed this week. Which of these do you most readily identify with? In the past, have you sought in what ways to become more righteous through these faulty approaches?

_____

_____

_____

Romans 5:19

Consider the following passages:

Romans 5:19. *"As through the one man's disobedience the many were made sinners, even so through the obedience of the One the many will be made righteous."*

IN ADAM: What happened?	IN CHRIST: What happened?
When did it happen?	When did it happen?

Romans 6:1-7

Romans 6:1-7. *"What shall we say then? Are we to continue in sin so that grace may increase? May it never be! How shall we who died to sin still live in it? Or do you not know that all of us who have been baptized into Christ Jesus have been baptized into His death? Therefore we have been buried with Him through baptism into death, so that as Christ was raised from the dead through the glory of the Father, so we too might walk in newness of life. For if we have become united with Him in the likeness of His death, certainly we shall also be in the likeness of His resurrection, knowing this, that our old self was crucified with Him, in order that our body of sin might be done away with, so that we would no longer be slaves to sin; for he who has died is freed from sin."*

1. Underline the words that tell what happened to you when you became a Christian.

2. What is Paul's answer to the charge that teaching pure grace might encourage people to become careless about sin?

_____

3. What was crucified with Jesus Christ, and what is the corresponding result?

_____

4. What words would you use to describe the person you were before you became a Christian?

_____

_____

What words would you use to describe yourself now?

_____

_____

_____

_____

End your study time this week affirming the truth of your identity in a prayer to your heavenly Father that thanks Him for taking away your old life and giving you a new life.

YOU DON'T HAVE
AN EVIL TWIN LIVING
INSIDE YOU

Last week you learned you have a brand-new nature, the very nature of Jesus Christ. This new nature was given to you at salvation. Within you is the very righteousness of Jesus Christ. So what happened to the old person you were before you became a Christian? That is what we are going to study this week.

Day One

For a long time I felt like I had a counterpart personality living inside me. It was as if there was an evil twin in me—Evil Steve, the one who wanted to come out and do the things that Saint Steve *could but never would do*. I tried to suppress this imaginary villain, to keep him quiet as much as possible. But every now and then, I would think he'd break out. And when he did, it wasn't a pretty sight. Sometimes he would yell at my kids, or entertain lustful thoughts, or lose his temper with my wife. At other times, it wouldn't be so dramatic. He would just lull me into a "who cares" attitude that caused me to stop reading the Bible, praying, and all the other things that Saint Steve would normally do.

It was only when I understood my identity in Christ that I realized this fact: There *is* no evil twin! He is only a phantom. He doesn't exist anymore. Understanding that truth caused me to experience greater freedom and victory than I had ever known in my Christian life.

Have you felt like you have an evil twin living inside you? Describe him. What does he look like?

_____

_____

_____

_____

I have good news for you about the twin you think you see. He's dead. Now, before we move any further, you need to reaffirm something about your core beliefs.

_____ Do you believe the Bible?

_____ Will you believe the Bible if it says something different from what you've always believed in the past?

_____ How about if the Bible says something different from what you feel or believe is true based on your own experiences? Does the Bible take authority over your emotions and experiences?

Good! Because I'm going to show you some Bible truths this week that may totally change some things you have believed in the past. That was the effect the verses we will study had on my life.

This week we're going to look at our old man, which the Scripture says is dead. Don't run ahead in your mind and ask, *If my old man is dead, why do I still sin?* We are going to answer that question next week. But for now, let's take it a step at a time. I want to establish this week that the person you were before you knew Christ died with Him—and that you don't have an evil twin living inside you.

My Old Man

Our old man is the identity we inherited from Adam. All of us were born "in Adam." Spiritually speaking, we were sinners before we were even born. Many people think they became sinners the first time they committed a sin, but that is not what the Scripture tells us.

Think about your own life for a moment. Can you remember the first time you ever committed a sin as a child? What was that sin?

_____

Who taught you how to do that?

_____

> You sin because you are a sinner. You are born with a sin nature.

I'm guessing that you answered "nobody." If you're like most children, your sin was probably lying or throwing a temper tantrum, or something like that. Where did that come from?

The Scripture says that we were sinners before we ever showed up on planet Earth. In fact, Romans 5:12 says it like this:

Romans 5:12

Just as through one man sin entered into the world, and death through sin, and so death spread to all men, because all sinned.

The reason you and I were born sinners is because we were born "in Adam," and when he sinned in the garden, we became sinners.

You don't become a sinner the first time you ever sin. You are not a sinner because you sin. Instead, you sin because you are a sinner. You are born with a sin nature. Because we are born with a nature to sin, the first time we ever sin we do so because we are sinners. So you might ask, "What must a person do to become a sinner?" The answer is very clear. What a person must do to become a sinner is to be born. When you showed up on this earth you were a sinner. It was your nature. It was in your spiritual DNA.

Psalm 58:3

Read Psalm 58:3. In your own words, write what that verse is teaching:

_____

Condemned from the Start

We were already in trouble when we showed up on planet Earth. We were born condemned to hell. The Bible says that "the judgment arose from one transgression resulting in condemnation" (Romans 5:16). We were born already condemned.

Most people are familiar with John 3:16: "God so loved the world, that He gave His only begotten Son, that whoever believes in Him shall not perish, but have eternal life." But do you know John 3:18? "He who does not believe has been judged already, because he has not believed in the name of the only begotten Son of God." When we are born, we are judged—condemned—already. We are born into this world condemned to hell. What does a person have to do to go to hell? Nothing. All you have to do is be born and do nothing, and you will go to hell. We are born headed for hell.

> *We were already in trouble when we showed up on planet Earth.*

Thoroughbred Sinners

Then the Scripture tells us that because we were born with a sin nature, our lifestyle was animated by a sin-filled spirit. Remember that your spirit is the core of your identity. Whatever you are in your spirit, that's who you are. When we were born, our spirit was filled with sin, so our identity was that we were sinners. We had a sin nature; it was our nature to sin.

In Ephesians 2:1-3, Paul put it like this:

> *You were dead in your trespasses and sins, in which you formerly walked according to the course of this world,*

according to the prince of the power of the air, of the spirit that is now working in the sons of disobedience. Among them we too all formerly lived in the lusts of our flesh, indulging the desires of the flesh and of the mind, and were by nature children of wrath, even as the rest.

You acted like what you were by nature. Before you met Christ, it was your nature to sin. You had one nature, and it was a sin nature. That's why you sinned. Sinners sin because it is their nature to sin. When you're a sinner, that is the job description. That's what you do. You sin. You have no choice about it. That old nature, that sin nature, is the source of all your actions.

How would you define a sinner?

Why does a sinner sin?

How does a sinner become a sinner?

Yesterday you saw that you were born a sinner. You were born in the line of Adam and you had a sin nature. But you are not an unsaved person today. You are a believer. You have experienced a radical transformation.

How did this transformation take place? It was by the cross of Jesus. There, the old man that you were in Adam died with Jesus. When Jesus died, your old nature died with him. Prayerfully study the following passages:

Romans 6:1-3. *"What shall we say then? Are we to continue in sin so that grace may increase? May it never be! How shall we who died to sin still live in it? Or do you not know that all of us who have been baptized into Christ Jesus have been baptized into His death?"*

Paul is saying, "Don't you get it? Don't you understand? When you were placed into Jesus Christ, you became a participant in His death. You were baptized into—immersed into, placed into—His death. You were crucified with Him."

Romans 6:6. *"Our old self was crucified with Him, in order that our body of sin might be done away with, so that we would no longer be slaves to sin; for he who has died is freed from sin."*

Read the verse again. What happened to your old self? It was crucified in order that our body of sin might be

_____

The source for sin in our lives was "done away with."

There it is, in the Bible. Do you believe it?

Romans 6:1-3

Romans 6:6

Colossians 3:3

Colossians 3:3. *"You have died and your life is hidden with Christ in God."* We all know Jesus died on the cross, but did you know that you died on the cross too? The old person you were in Adam died. We were placed into Christ on the cross and our old self died with Him. That old sin nature died with Jesus Christ.

Write out Colossians 3:3 from at least two different translations.

_____

_____

_____

_____

_____

_____

_____

You might be wondering, *How could I die with Jesus on the cross when I was not born until many centuries later?* Remember that God stands above time. You and I understand reality based on time. But because God is above time, He sees from beginning to end at one glance.

So God, who is not bound by time, took the person you were—the sinner you were—and placed you into Jesus Christ on the cross. When He died, you died with Him. Then you were born again.

When you were born again, you were given a brand-new nature. The old you died. You were crucified with Jesus and no longer have life independent of Him. Now He is your very life. The old you is gone forever. The old you is dead.

Before you were saved, how many natures did you have? You had one nature. It was a sin nature. That nature was crucified. It is dead. You were born again with a new nature. How many natures do you have now? You have one nature—the nature of Jesus Christ. I know this contradicts what many of us have always believed, what we have been taught. But I'm asking you again, do you believe the Bible? What does the Bible say? The Bible says our old man died.

You have one nature—the nature of Jesus Christ.

If it was not your old nature that died, then what did die? What is the Bible talking about? Something died. What was it? Not your body. Not your soul, your personality. It was your old sin nature.

I know our experience seems to contradict this truth. You may feel you still have a bent toward sin. We'll discuss the reason for this fact next week, but let's just build the case a step at a time. The Bible says that your sin nature died. It is no more. If you still sin, there must be some reason other than that your old sin nature causes it.

Paul states this truth in emphatic and radical terms in Galatians 2:20:

Galatians 2:20

I have been crucified with Christ; and it is no longer I who live, but Christ lives in me; and the life which I now live in the flesh I live by faith in the Son of God, who loved me and gave Himself up for me.

Paul says, "I died. I no longer live." Jesus Christ is not "in your life." You no longer have a life of your own. Jesus Christ *is* your life.

Read the following Scriptures and underline the words and phrases that tell you Jesus is the only life you have.

Acts 17:28

In Him we live and move and exist (Acts 17:28).

Colossians 3:4

When Christ, who is your life, appears, then you also will appear with him in glory (Colossians 3:4).

Philippians 1:21-22

To me, to live is Christ and to die is gain (Philippians 1:21-22).

> *God doesn't just clear the cobwebs out of your soul. By the cross, God kills the spider.*

The old man died. I have a new nature. Jesus is my very life. If you believe the Bible, you have to believe that. If this does not agree with what you have believed in the past, your brain might be scrambling right now trying to put it all together. I know when I first saw that the Scripture clearly states my old nature is dead, I said, "That can't be true. I know me." But now I would say, "No, I didn't know me. But thank God, *He* knew me. He told me the truth about myself." Our identity as a sinner was removed from us by the cross. It's gone.

Let me illustrate it like this. When I was a kid, I used to hear people talking about revival coming. They said it would be like God clearing the spiderwebs out of our souls. And so every time we would have revival services, we would attend hoping that God was going to clear the cobwebs out of our souls. But here is the good news the Bible teaches: God doesn't just clear the cobwebs out of your soul. By the cross, God kills the spider.

Your sin nature is dead. Gone. No longer lives. How can you know that? The Bible tells you so. Let the Word of God be the determining factor in your doctrine and belief, not what your experience tells you or your observations suggest.

Are you convinced that the New Testament teaches that your old man, your sin nature, is dead?

_____

Do you choose to believe what the Bible clearly and consistently teaches?

_____

Three passages of Scripture have been our focus today. Read those passages again slowly, asking the Holy Spirit to show you what it means when it talks about the fact that we died. You will come to see that the old man that you may have believed was an evil twin living inside you is dead.

If you recognize this truth as a reality, fill in the death certificate below. If not, come back to it when the Holy Spirit has made you ready.

DEATH CERTIFICATE

For: _____

I have been crucified with Christ and I no longer live. The old nature that gave me my identity has been put to death on the cross of Jesus Christ.

Signed: _____

Date: _____

Galatians 2:20

Colossians 2:11

Let's come back today to Galatians 2:20. I love this passage. It lays bare the lie that keeps us enslaved—the lie that we have two natures, one good and one bad, pulling against each another. The old nature was put to death. Paul said, "I no longer live." The old man he was before he met Jesus Christ had died. Now he was a completely different person. The same happened to you when you trusted Christ! Let's continue our study today with additional verses that show the evil twin is dead.

In Him you were also circumcised with a circumcision made without hands, in the removal of the body of the flesh by the circumcision of Christ (Colossians 2:11).

It doesn't get any clearer in Scripture than this illustration of circumcision. That happens when skin is cut away from a man at the place on his body from which life originates. When that piece of skin is cut away, it never grows back. Circumcision was the covenant sign that God had with His people in the Old Testament. Every man acknowledged God's covenant with him in that way.

In the new covenant, God still uses circumcision as a sign of His covenant with us, although it isn't physical circumcision anymore. Colossians 2:11 explains that God has performed a circumcision on us as His covenant sign with us. This circumcision is different from the old covenant circumcision because it is performed without hands.

What God has miraculously done is to reach down inside of you and cut away the source from which your old life was generated. He has circumcised you spiritually. He has removed the old nature, the source of your old life. The Bible says it's never going to grow back. You are not a sinner saved by grace. The nature that made you a sinner has been cut away. You are a saint. Don't call yourself a sinner anymore. I'm not suggesting that you never sin anymore, but that your identity as a sinner has been removed by the cross.

> *Do you not know that the unrighteous will not inherit the kingdom of God? Do not be deceived; neither fornicators, nor idolaters, nor adulterers, nor effeminate, nor homosexuals, nor thieves, nor the covetous, nor drunkards, nor revilers, nor swindlers, will inherit the kingdom of God. Such were some of you; but you were washed, but you were sanctified, but you were justified in the name of the Lord Jesus Christ and in the Spirit of our God (1 Corinthians 6:9-11).*

> *Who you are and how you act may not always coincide, but that doesn't change the fact of who you are.*
>
> **1 Corinthians 6:9-11**

The old unrighteous you died, and now you are righteous. You're a saint who sometimes sins, but you are not a sinner. It's not your nature to sin. The Scripture says unrighteous people are not going to heaven. Are you righteous? Yes. How do you become righteous? You receive righteousness as a gift.

Who you are and how you act may not always coincide, but that doesn't change the fact of who you are. As an example, let me pull out a word from this passage—the word *drunkard*. It's the biblical word for alcoholic. Paul says that an alcoholic will not enter the kingdom of heaven.

You can't be a Christian and an alcoholic. I didn't say you can't become addicted to alcohol. You may have a propensity toward abusing alcohol, but that is not who you are. Abuse of alcohol may be your flesh pattern, but it is not who you are. You have a new identity if you have received Christ. We don't wear the disgraceful identity of the past like a shameful badge of dishonor.

When a Christian person says of himself or herself, "I'm an alcoholic," it is not the truth. Maybe it would be more truthful to say, "Hi, I'm _____, and I'm a saint who sometimes has a severe inclination toward drunkenness."

What if we expected everyone to identify himself by his flesh pattern. Imagine that—"Hello, my name is Sue and I'm a gossip. It's been three days since I've told anything juicy about anybody." Or, "Hello, my name is John and I'm a lust-filled man. It's been a week since I've had an inappropriate fantasy." It would be ridiculous to identify ourselves by our sinful flesh patterns, because that is not who we are anymore.

> *You have a new identity if you have received Christ.*

You are not an alcoholic if you are a Christian. You can act that way if you choose, but it isn't who you are. Sometimes when I'm sick, my wife will say, "When you're sick, you sure are a big baby." I might answer, "I am not! I have my birth certificate to prove I'm not a baby." You see, I'm not a baby, but I can act like one sometimes.

Who you are and how you act might be two different things. Can a Christian act like an alcoholic? Yes. Can he act like an adulterer? Can he act like a swindler? Of course. But remember, your identity is not determined by what you do. Your identity is determined by your birth. If you've been born again, the old sinner you were before has died and you have been born as a saint. You're not who you were. So don't appropriate the sins of your past as part of your identity now. They aren't.

You're a new person, a new creation. This new man has died to everything he or she inherited from Adam. When you were in Adam, you had Adam's family traits. Now, you have new family traits.

Have you ever noticed that family members tend to look alike? My children have the traits and the appearance of me. They look like me because they were born into my family.

When we were born into the family of Adam, we looked like that family. It was the sinner family. We had all the family traits. But now we've been born into the family of Jesus Christ and we look like the family of God. The old person you were has died. You have died to the characteristics of Adam's family.

What were the characteristics of Adam's family? The major characteristic was a nature that was totally depraved. Before a person comes to know Christ, that person is rotten to the core. He is spiritually dead. The best deeds he can do are an offense to the perfectly righteous God. But you and I, having been born again, don't have that old depraved nature now. We are dead to depravity and sin and we are alive to righteousness.

The Lie That Keeps Us Enslaved

The "evil twin" lie held me at a standstill in my spiritual life for a long time. I thought I had a good side and a bad side. There was a part of me that had a hunger to live a godly lifestyle, but I saw another part of me that hungered to live in ungodly ways. I thought I was righteous and unrighteous at the same time.

I even told an illustration about two dogs who fought each other all the time. I used to tell people those two dogs were like your two natures. They're battling. I used to say, "The way you can determine which one wins is that you feed the good dog and you starve the bad dog. And as you starve the bad dog, he'll get weaker and weaker; as you feed the good dog, he'll get stronger and stronger, then he'll defeat the bad dog." I would often give people a list of things to do to feed the good dog. Then I'd give them a list of things you can't do or you'll be feeding the bad dog. Two natures at war—that's what I believed. The problem with the story is that it communicates a lie. In reality that bad dog has been killed. He was run over by the cross. He is not alive anymore.

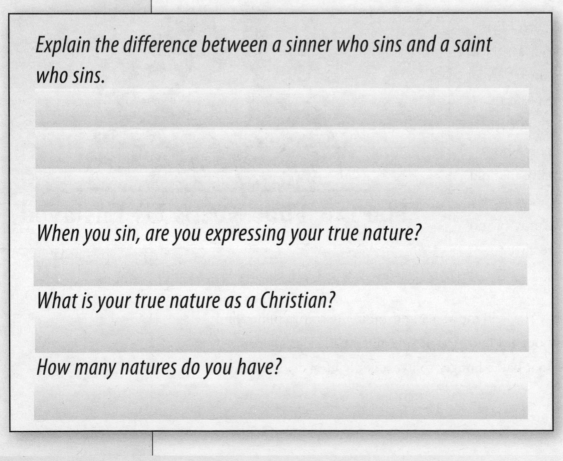

Explain the difference between a sinner who sins and a saint who sins.

When you sin, are you expressing your true nature?

What is your true nature as a Christian?

How many natures do you have?

Yesterday you learned that the person you were before you received Christ is no longer alive. I know this may be hard for some people to accept. After all, our experience doesn't seem to validate this fact. The teaching many of us have received in church contradicts the idea that our old nature died. Our feelings tell us it can't be so.

Day Four

But I want to point you back to the Bible again. Study and meditate on the verses we have examined. For me there had to be a complete paradigm shift to be able to accept the truth that my old nature was dead. It didn't seem possible. The truth didn't agree with what I had been taught or had believed, felt, or seemed to experience. But it was in the Bible. Finally, I was forced to respond, "Lord, I don't understand *how* it can be true that my old man died, but Your Word says that's the way it is, so I believe it!" That was a turning point for me.

Don't worry about not having all your questions answered yet about why you still sin. Those answers will come. For now, ask yourself the question, *What does the Bible say about this?* If you see it in the Bible, then believe it whether it makes sense to you or not. Sometimes we must rise above our upbringing, our church tradition, our feelings and personal experience, and just rest our faith on the Word of God. Will you do that?

_____

What is the greatest barrier in your mind that might prevent you from accepting the truth that your old nature died with Jesus on the cross?

_____

_____

If you are struggling with the idea that your old man died, will you pause in your study right now and pray? Stop studying and talk to your heavenly Father about it. Jesus promised that the Holy Spirit would guide us into *all* truth, and this is an important truth you need to appropriate by faith. If you aren't struggling with this truth, but fully accept it, then you can skip the prayer that follows and press on in your study.

Otherwise, maybe this suggested prayer will help get you started:

Heavenly Father,

If this idea about my old nature being dead is true, I want to understand it. The thing I'm struggling with concerning this idea is... (tell Him what your struggle is). Right now I lay aside any misplaced confidence I may have in what I've been taught or believed in the past. I lay aside the right to base my beliefs on what I feel or on my own track record with sin in my life. I don't want to try to rationalize my way through this. I want to study Your Word and come to the truth that You reveal to me. I'm sincerely open, so show me the truth. I'm trusting You to do that, and I thank You now for Your guidance.

In Jesus' name, amen.

Now sign your name to this prayer to own it:

Implications of a Dead Old Man

The Bible teaches that there are tremendous benefits associated with the fact that our old nature was put to death with Jesus on the cross. Perhaps the greatest blessing of our co-crucifixion with Christ is given in Romans 6:7: "He who has died is freed from sin."

Romans 6:7

How would you define the word "free"?

_____

Did you die with Jesus Christ?

_____

Where does that leave you in relation to sin?

_____

That's right, free! The Bible teaches that because of the death of our old nature, sin has no more power over us. We have been set free from its tyrannical rule in our lives. When we trusted Christ, for the first time we were free to live a righteous lifestyle, out from under the cruel influence of sin in our lives.

You don't have to sin anymore for one simple reason—you are dead! Dead men don't sin. Let me give an example.

Imagine Leo overdosing on cocaine and dying. They take his body to the funeral home and prepare it for burial. A few hours before the funeral starts, one of his drug buddies comes into the parlor where they have Leo's corpse laid out. Nobody else is in the room, so his buddy walks over to the casket and leans over. "Hey, Leo," he says. "We're alone right now, man. I've got some good stuff here in my pocket." He reaches into his pocket and pulls out a small bag with cocaine in it. "Look man, it's pure. Take a snort," he says, while putting the bag under Leo's nose. "What's your problem, man? Here, I'll put a little on my finger for you to taste. You'll see, it's good stuff."

Do you know what Leo is doing all the time this is going on? Just lying there. If Leo could speak at that moment, do you know what he would say? "Hey, stupid! I'm dead! Can't you see that?" Dead men don't want cocaine, even if they loved it before.

The Bible clearly teaches that a part of our inheritance is that we have *died* to sin. You can sin if you choose, but when you understand your new identity you will discover that you don't *want* to live in sin anymore. You died to all that. Now you are alive to God. He motivates your desires and interests. You finally have power over sin!

Balancing the Books

Consider Romans 6:11: "Even so consider yourselves to be dead to sin, but alive to God in Christ Jesus." Let's pause and examine closely the word "consider" in this verse. The word is translated as "reckon" in the old King James Bible and is a financial term.

Romans 6:11

You may not be interested in the original Greek language of the Bible, but I'm going to offer some information here for those who may want to dig a little deeper. Like many in ministry, I studied Greek, but make no claims to being proficient at it. This one is a no-brainer, though. You can get this kind of information from many places on the Internet. I found the information in the next few paragraphs at crosswalk.com. I'm offering this information to show you that there is *solid* biblical proof that your old nature died with Christ. Study this for yourself until you are persuaded.

> *You finally have power over sin!*

The word "consider" is the Greek word *logizomai*. It means "to compute, to count, to calculate" something. To reckon your bank statement is to find out the bottom-line balance in your account after reconciling all the facts about activity in the account.

The *KJV New Testament Greek Lexicon* says this about the matter:

> *This word deals with reality. If I "logizomai" or "reckon" that my bankbook has $25 in it, it has $25 in it. Otherwise I am deceiving myself. This word refers to facts, not suppositions.*

What practical application does that have in your life as a Christian? It means that the authority sin had over your life in the past is done now. That isn't a theoretical possibility, it is a fact. Its power over you has been emptied. There's nothing left in the bank. It's a dead account. God closed your sin account when you died with Christ at the cross. You have a new account now. Your investments rest in the life of Jesus now. You haven't diversified. You've put all your eggs in one basket, and it is Him.

1 Timothy 1:12

Paul said it like this: "I know whom I have believed and I am convinced that He is able to guard what I have entrusted [literally "deposited"] to Him until that day" (1 Timothy 1:12). Paul was saying, "I've opened a new account now. The only deposits I have anymore are in Christ and I *know whom I have believed.*"

Romans 6:14

Paul was clear about whom He believed. Are you clear on that matter? Do you believe that by the cross, God emptied the sin account and that you have no relationship to it anymore?

When Corrie ten Boom was imprisoned with her sister Betsie in a Nazi concentration camp during World War II, the Lord spoke to Betsie one day and told her that by the new year they both would be free. Free from the cruel tyranny of the guards who tormented them daily.

By the time the new year came, Betsie had died. Was she free from the power of the cruel guards? Of course she was. That's what happened to you. Sin controlled you before you knew Christ, but because you died with Him, it has no power over you anymore. Paul wrote in Romans 6:14 that "sin shall not be master over you, for you are not under law, but under grace." By God's grace, you have been set free from sin's authority through your own death.

As we come to the conclusion of our study this week, it is my prayer that you have appropriated the truth of the death of your old sin nature. To bypass this truth is like neglecting to touch third base on your way to home plate—it's not going to work. Understanding the death of our old man is the key to appropriating and living out of our new identity in Jesus Christ.

Day Five

If you did have two natures living inside you simultaneously, then you would be in trouble, because Jesus said that a house divided against itself *cannot* stand. If you are going to stand strong and experience the grace walk to the fullest, it is necessary to agree with God about what He says concerning the death of your old man. There is no shortcut on this one.

To conclude the study of this week's truth that you don't have an evil twin living inside you, I'm going to ask you to review the things you've studied about it. Normally, to be redundant in a book of any kind is a bad thing. However, I feel so strongly about the importance of you locking in on this truth that I want to walk you through a short review for the purpose of allowing you to deeply assimilate the things you have considered this week.

There are several key passages and points from your study this week that I want you to review. Be sure to write down your answers to the questions asked in your study today so you can solidify and internalize your belief on this matter. Don't skim over this material. Renewing the mind is important and often involves *unlearning* as much as it involves learning. If the idea that your old nature is dead is a new idea to you, you need this review to replace old, faulty beliefs with new, biblical ones.

Consider some of the verses you have studied this week and respond to the questions about each one. (Answers will be given at the end of today's study.)

Romans 5:12

Just as through one man sin entered into the world, and death through sin, and so death spread to all men, because all sinned (Romans 5:12).

1. Who was the "one man" who caused sin to enter the world?

_____

2. What does a person have to do to become a sinner?

_____

Ephesians 2:1-3

You were dead in your trespasses and sins, in which you formerly walked according to the course of this world, according to the prince of the power of the air, of the spirit that is now working in the sons of disobedience. Among them we too all formerly lived in the lusts of our flesh, indulging the desires of the flesh and of the mind, and were by nature children of wrath, even as the rest (Ephesians 2:1-3).

3. What was your spiritual condition before you became a Christian?

_____

4. How does this verse describe your identity as far as your nature is concerned?

_____

This verse says that you were "even as the rest." In other words, you were in the same boat with everybody else outside Christ.

Our old self was crucified with Him, in order that our body of sin might be done away with, so that we would no longer be slaves to sin; for he who has died is freed from sin (Romans 6:6).

Romans 6:6

5. What part of you was your "old self"? (Other translations call it the old man or our sinful selves.)

_____

_____

6. What was the result of our old self being crucified with Jesus Christ?

_____

_____

7. Why are you now able to live free from sin?

_____

_____

I have been crucified with Christ; and it is no longer I who live, but Christ lives in me; and the life which I now live in the flesh I live by faith in the Son of God, who loved me and gave Himself up for me (Galatians 2:20).

Galatians 2:20

8. What does Paul mean when he says, "I no longer live, but Christ lives in me"?

_____

_____

9. How then are we able to live our lives if we "no longer live"?

_____

Colossians 2:11

In Him you were also circumcised with a circumcision made without hands, in the removal of the body of the flesh by the circumcision of Christ (Colossians 2:11).

10. In what way does circumcision reflect what God has done to you at the moment you became a Christian?

_____

_____

11. Exactly what did God cut away from you when you were saved?

_____

_____

Romans 6:11

Consider yourselves to be dead to sin, but alive to God in Christ Jesus (Romans 6:11).

12. What does the word "consider" mean in this verse?

_____

_____

13. What is the relationship you have to sin now that you are a Christian?

_____

_____

Thank God, our old man is dead. Thank God, we were crucified with Christ.

Would you appropriate this truth by faith right now? As you end this week's study, pray in your own words and affirm to your heavenly Father that you believe this truth. Don't worry about not understanding everything or having every question answered at this point. Just thank Him that He put to death the old person you were and has made you a new creature in Christ.

Answers to the questions in this section

1. Adam.
2. Nothing. Just be born.
3. Dead.
4. I was a child of wrath, not a child of God.
5. My sin nature.
6. I am no longer a slave to sin.
7. I died with Christ, so sin lost its power over me.
8. The old me is dead and now Jesus is my very life.
9. By trusting Jesus to live His life through me.
10. He cut away the source of sin within me.
11. My old sin nature.
12. It means to calculate it to be so in the way one finds an accurate bank balance.
13. I am dead to sin and have no relationship to it anymore.

5

You Can
Overcome Temptation
by Understanding
Why You Sin

The truth we will examine now brings us to a focal point in experiencing the grace walk. During your study this week, you will learn the answer to the often asked question, "If our old man is dead, and if we have the very nature of Jesus Christ, why is it that we still sin?" This is the thing that makes it hard for many people to believe their old sin nature is dead. After all, they can look at their lives and they see that they still sometimes sin.

So the question naturally follows, "If I'm righteous, why do I still commit unrighteous acts? If I have only the nature of Christ, why do I sin? And what can I do about it?"

Those are the very issues you will have answered this week. You are going to learn two important aspects of overcoming temptation. One has to do with the residual effects of sin in your physical body (*why* you sin) and the other will equip you to say a victorious "No!" to temptation when it comes to you.

Let's begin our study this week with a foundational passage on the subject of sin's influence in the life of a Christian. We will start by carefully examining Romans 7:16-23. Go through this passage slowly twice, each time looking at it from a different angle. First, underline every phrase that tells you that sin is repulsive to Paul. Next, circle every phrase that tells you Paul is attracted to righteousness.

> *If I do the very thing I do not want to do, I agree with the Law, confessing that the Law is good. So now, no longer am I the one doing it, but sin which dwells in me. For I know that nothing good dwells in me, that is, in my flesh; for the willing is present in me, but the doing of the good is not. For the good that I want, I do not do, but I practice the very evil that I do not want.*

Day One

Romans 7:16-23

But if I am doing the very thing I do not want, I am no longer the one doing it, but sin which dwells in me.

I find then the principle that evil is present in me, the one who wants to do good. For I joyfully concur with the law of God in the inner man, but I see a different law in the members of my body, waging war against the law of my mind and making me a prisoner of the law of sin which is in my members.

In the passage above, Paul describes what it looks like when a person *tries* to experience victory over sin. When you read this description of trying to overcome sin, you see that sin was repulsive to Paul. Sin is repulsive to every child of God. It is the nature of the Christian to hate sin.

You have the very nature of Jesus Christ. If you didn't hate sin, you wouldn't give it a thought when you commit sin. The reason you experience internal conflict when you commit sin is because in your spirit you hate it. If you didn't hate it, there would be no conflict—sin would come naturally to you. Even if you feel enslaved to a sin, even if it gratifies you, that doesn't mean you love it.

The fact that sin is pleasurable doesn't say something about you. It says something about sin. Sin is pleasurable many times. That's an objective fact. If it weren't pleasurable, there would be no enticement to it. The pleasure of sin is *for a season,* but the pleasure may be there nonetheless.

When a person is operating under legalism, he will often try to stop committing a certain sin because he is convinced this specific sin is his problem. Really, that sin isn't the problem at all. That specific sin is just a symptom of the problem. Someone has said, "Your main problem is that you think your problem is your problem. But your problem is not your problem at all, and that's your problem."

Do you think the specific sins in your life are your main problem? They aren't. The real problem is that sin occurs when a Christian functions out of his flesh. That's your real problem. What you do—the sin you commit—is the symptom of the problem. The problem is that you are living out of your flesh when you commit sins. The real sin is independent living.

> *The mother of all sins is independent living.*

The mother of all sins is independent living. Sin occurs when a Christian functions out of his or her flesh. Remember, your flesh is not who you are, but only how you function when you fail to depend upon Jesus as your life source.

Make no mistake about it, sin is repulsive to the Christian. To experience the grace walk it is important to renew your mind and stop saying things like, "But I love my sin. That's why I do it." When you say that you are affirming a lie. If the truth will set you free, what will lies do to you? Put you in bondage! You don't love your sin.

Romans 7:16-23

Look back at the text in Romans 7:16-23 and note each time the apostle Paul uses the personal pronoun "I." Read the text, inserting your name every time he uses the word "I" as if the passage were being written about you. Read it out loud if possible.

Deep within his heart, does the person in the text love sin or hate it?

_____

_____

Is this person evil or does he simply recognize that there is something evil within himself?

_____

_____

Deep within his "inner man" (his true self), what is the attitude of this Christian toward the ways of God?

_____

_____

What is the source of sin within the life of the person the passage describes?

_____

_____

Maybe you've always seen the negative aspects of this passage when you have read it before now. Do you see that Paul actually reveals his faith right in the midst of his expression of his failures? He hungered for God's ways to be fulfilled in his life. He hated the sins that caused him to stumble. He recognized that when he sinned, it wasn't his true self.

Think about the sin that most often causes you to stumble in your own life. In the space below, write a detailed description of how you feel about the sin. Don't write how you feel about *yourself* after you've committed the sin, but how you feel about the sin itself.

If you want to experience the grace walk, stop believing the lie that you love your sins. You don't. You hate them. Otherwise you wouldn't even want to study a book like this. As you end today's study, pray and tell your heavenly Father how you feel about your sins. Lay them out before Him without trying to hide any part of them.

Be completely honest about your situation. If it *feels* like you still love your sins, tell God so. If you have believed you can't be set free, acknowledge that fact. Then ask Him to reveal to you how you can find freedom from the sins that haunt you.

Finally, by faith, express your love and appreciation to Him for the victory over your sins that the Bible teaches is possible because of the cross. You don't need to understand *how* to experience freedom over your sins in order to praise Him for the freedom made possible through the cross. Just thank Him by faith. In the days ahead, you will learn how to appropriate the power of the cross to find the freedom you so desire.

Yesterday you discovered that you don't love the sins you commit. You hate them. That's why you experience a negative response inwardly after you have committed a sin.

Having established that your attitude toward your sins is one of hatred, I want you to see today why you still sometimes sin. Look again today at Romans 7. We will consider verses 16-17 and 20:

Day Two

> *If I do the very thing I do not want to do, I agree with the Law, confessing that the Law is good. So now, no longer am I the one doing it, but sin which dwells in me...But if I am doing the very thing I do not want, I am no longer the one doing it, but sin which dwells in me.*

Romans 7:16-17,20

Twice in three verses the apostle Paul says, "When I sin, I am no longer the one doing it. It is the sin which indwells me." He speaks here of what many call "indwelling sin." Where is this indwelling sin? In verse 23, Paul says it is "in my body."

Romans 7:23

The Bible is teaching here that we, as Christians, do still have indwelling sin within us. Indwelling sin is *in* you, but it is not *you*. It's not who you are. Your spirit has been completely redeemed and sanctified. Your soul is being sanctified. But we all know we don't have glorified bodies yet. We have the same body we had before we were saved. It is within this body that indwelling sin resides.

Paul says that when he sins, he is not the one doing it. What are we to make of this statement? Is he shirking responsibility for his sin? Is he saying, "It's not my fault I sinned. The devil made me do it"? No, not at all. He is not advocating that we should shirk responsibility. Make no mistake—when you sin, it didn't just happen. You made a choice. What Paul is saying is, when we sin, it is not consistent with who we are and we are not acting out of our true identity. It's not *me* when I sin, because that's not who I am. The source of sin in my life is *in* me, but is not *me*.

Romans 7:21

Many people believe that the fact they still sin proves that they are still evil, that they still have that sin nature. But Paul didn't think of himself as an evil man. Look in verse 21. He wrote, "I find then the principle that evil is *present in me*."

Sin Is in Me, but Is Not Me

Think of a man having an operation. Imagine that the surgeon, during the course of the operation, puts four sponges in the man to absorb fluids. At the end of the operation, the surgeon removes three sponges, but he accidentally leaves one sponge behind inside the man. He sews him up with that sponge in him. A few days later, the surgeon checks on the man to see how he's doing. The patient says, "Doctor, something is wrong with me! Since you operated on me, I have had an insatiable thirst. I can't get enough water! Another thing, since the surgery I have not emptied my bladder once. I think something is wrong with me!"

So the doctor sends him for X-rays to determine what is wrong with him. After examining the X-rays, the doctor comes to the man's bedside and sheepishly admits, "Sir, there's not something wrong *with* you. There's something wrong *in* you." Do you see my point? The power of sin is *in* you, but it is not *you*.

I had a kidney stone earlier this year and had to have it surgically removed, but I didn't begin to call myself "Rocky" because I had a kidney stone in my body. It wasn't me. It was only in me.

I'm not sure where in your body the power of sin is. Maybe it's in your brain. Your brain is like a computer. It has many files stored. You don't necessarily run all the files, but they're there somewhere on your hard drive. Maybe all those flesh patterns and ways of operating are stored somewhere in your brain. Then, when we're not trusting Jesus to live His life through us, those files are activated. When we're not abiding in Christ, the power of indwelling sin activates those flesh files and we act out of our flesh. The power of sin is in my body. Sin is present in me.

> *When we're not abiding in Christ, the power of indwelling sin activates those flesh files and we act out of our flesh.*

Notice in this text how Paul separates the power of sin from his identity. "No longer am I the one doing it," he says. Paul is saying, "Here is my behavior, these are my personal actions—I am doing the very things I hate!" Let me ask you, does that sound like a man who loves his sin? He did not. When you sin, it is a contradiction of who you are.

Sin is resident in the Christian's body. Indwelling sin is in you, but it is not you. Indwelling sin does seek to overtake you and control you if you let that happen by not trusting Christ to be your life source. You aren't a bad person just because something bad is inside you!

Describe the meaning of "indwelling sin."

_____

_____

How does this understanding change how you perceive your sinful behavior?

_____

_____

Understanding the presence of indwelling sin within you is a key to finding freedom over sins. It isn't because it is still your nature to sin that you still commit sins. It is because of indwelling sin that is not *you*, but rather resides in your body. We'll study more later this week about how indwelling sin can cause you to become deceived and yield to temptation, but for now I want you to see that indwelling sin isn't indicative of who you are as a person. It has nothing to do with your basic nature.

People often struggle with the idea that their old nature is dead because they mistakenly think that, when they see the presence of indwelling sin in themselves, they are seeing the old nature. It is important not to confuse the two. Consider the differences between the old nature you used to have and the indwelling sin that is still in you.

The Old Nature	*Indwelling Sin*
1. was crucified with Christ	*1. still resides within you*
2. gave you your identity	*2. is inside you, but has nothing whatsoever to do with who you are*
3. was in your spirit, the core of your being	*3. is in your body*

Does it matter if we understand the difference between our old nature and indwelling sin? Absolutely! Once you know that the problem within you is indwelling sin and that it isn't your own nature, you come to realize that you aren't your own worst enemy! You are a holy person who still lives in a human body that has the residual effect of the sin that once gave you your identity as a person. That's not true anymore. The old man is dead, and the indwelling sin that resides in the members of your body has nothing to do with your identity.

If we are holy, then why do we sin? It's because the power of indwelling sin lives within our bodies. This doesn't suggest it isn't our fault when we sin, but does suggest that it isn't our *nature* to sin any longer. This distinction is important because, to overcome the enemy, we must first understand who the enemy is and how he operates.

> I'll repeat it again for emphasis: You are not your own worst enemy. If you have been fighting against yourself in an effort to be victorious over temptation, it is no wonder you've been defeated. Now that you recognize who the enemy really is, you'll be in a position to learn how he works against you so you can learn to effectively resist temptation.

Day Three

Let's begin the study today with a True/False quiz to see how much you've learned about indwelling sin. Answer with "T" or "F" for each of the following statements:

1. _____ It isn't my fault when I commit a sin.

2. _____ The reason I sin is because I'm basically a bad person.

3. _____ My old sin nature still causes me to sin sometimes.

4. _____ Indwelling sin is not indicative of who I am.

5. _____ I am not my own worst enemy.

6. _____ Indwelling sin is in my body.

The first three statements above are false and the last three are true. We are responsible for it when we sin, but it doesn't mean we are a bad person. Our old sin nature died and, while indwelling sin is in our bodies, it is not the source of our identity. Therefore, we aren't our own worst enemy. Who we are is determined by what is in our spirits, and indwelling sin resides in our bodies, not our spirits.

So we have discovered that the culprit in temptation is indwelling sin, not ourselves. The enemy of our souls uses this indwelling sin to cause us to yield to sin. Having seen who the enemy is, let's consider today how he operates to pull us down.

How can he so effectively cause us to fall prey to this indwelling sin? He does it through the thoughts that come into our minds. My friend Bill Gillham taught me a lot about this matter. He explains how the enemy defeats us by disguising his voice when he entices us with temptation.

When the enemy comes, he speaks in first-person singular—"I"—so I think it's my own thoughts. In other words, he would never say, "Hey, Steve. Will you do a favor for me?" He knows I would recognize the source of that voice and immediately say no.

So he puts a thought in my mind and makes me think it is my own thought. I may have a thought like this: *I am sick and tired of the way my wife has been doing this. I'm going to let her have it.* Now, that's not my thought. It was planted in my mind in an attempt to fire up the old engines of indwelling sin.

It's not me who generated that thought, but it's there nonetheless. The thought continues, *That's right, I'm going to let her have it. I'm just going to tell her what I think about her stupid behavior.*

Then I have another thought: *No, wait a minute. I'm not going to do that. I'm not going to be mean to my wife over such a small thing as this.* That thought was mine. How do I know it's my thought? Because it is consistent with who I am to act lovingly toward my wife. But then another thought comes: *Well, but I'm just tired of this happening. And I've already told her not to do it. So I'm just going to go in there and tell her what I think about it.* Then I think, *No, I love Melanie. I'm not going to talk to her like that.*

Do you see what is going on? Right now, if I don't know the truth, I think I'm having an argument with myself. But I'm not. I'm having an argument with indwelling sin. If I don't know who I am in Christ, this thought may keep bombarding my mind: "Go in there and let her have it!" Finally I just give in to it. I give her a piece of my mind. Then immediately the thought floods my mind, *Oh, what a terrible husband I am! How could I speak to my wife that way?* Guess where that one came from!

Do you see how the enemy works? He'll inject thoughts into your mind and make them sound like yours. The power of indwelling sin will activate your flesh and you'll act out of that flesh. Then the enemy will turn around and condemn you for doing the very thing he convinced you to do. Who ever said the enemy fights fair?

> *Not every thought you have is your own. It is essential that you know this.*

Stop now and ask the Holy Spirit to bring to your mind what He wants you to see. Think through recent days or even recent hours. What thoughts have you had that enticed you to act from your flesh? Readjust your response to those thoughts as you recognize the truth about the power of indwelling sin. How does your perspective change?

Not every thought you have is your own. It is essential that you know this. Thoughts can be introduced into your mind that don't come from you. They don't belong to you.

You may be asking, "How do I know if a thought that comes to my mind is from Jesus, the devil, or me?" That's not a hard question to answer. If it is an unholy thought, that thought did not come from Jesus. If it is an unholy thought, that thought didn't come from you either. You are holy. You have a holy nature. Holy people do not generate unholy thoughts. If it's an unholy thought, you can know immediately where it came from.

"Okay," you might say, "but what if it's not an unholy thought? Is it my thought, or is it the thought of Jesus?" And the answer is, "Yes." It is *our* thought. The Scripture tells us we have the mind of Christ. Not only can Jesus live through you, He can *think* through you. We have fallen into the error of believing that there are three kinds of thoughts: holy thoughts, unholy thoughts, and just regular thoughts. But that's not true. Consider this example:

Check the statement you think would be the most holy thought.

☐ I think I'm going to take my son on a mission trip with me.

☐ I think I'm going to take my son to a ball game.

It's a trick question. You should have checked both, because they are both equally holy. Without a doubt, one thought is more *religious* than the other, but both thoughts are holy. Do you know why? Because Jesus can live through me at a ball game just as well as He can live through me on a mission trip.

> **When you're abiding in Christ, every thought you have is a holy thought.**

When you're abiding in Christ, every thought you have is a holy thought. But not every thought that comes to you is your own. So when the power of indwelling sin introduces a thought, you take that thought captive to the obedience of Jesus Christ.

Consider the following scripture:

> *We are destroying speculations and every lofty thing raised up against the knowledge of God, and we are taking every thought captive to the obedience of Christ (2 Corinthians 10:5).*

2 Corinthians 10:5

How is Paul instructing us to deal with unholy thoughts? (Paraphrase his words.)

_____

_____

_____

What is the difference between having a thought that passes through your mind and acting on the thought?

_____

_____

I was trying to illustrate this concept to a man I was counseling. I was trying to get him to understand that not every thought a person has is his own. Sitting in on this counseling session was also a man named James, whom I was mentoring in how to counsel from a grace perspective. So I leaned forward to the man I was counseling and whispered to him so James could not hear, "Hit James in the face and knock him off that chair into the floor. It won't kill him. Do it!" The man was puzzled. He sat there trying to decide what to do. Finally I said, "Well, are you going to do it?"

> *Do you see? Not every thought you have comes from you.*

"No!" the man answered. "I'm not going to do it."

"Well, are you at least going to ask God to forgive you for having such a terrible thought?" I asked him.

"You're the one who said it!" replied the startled man.

Do you see? Not every thought you have comes from you. You are righteous. If you have an unrighteous thought, bring it into captivity to the obedience of Christ. I remember before I understood this truth that I would be praying and some ungodly thought would come into my head. I would stop praying and begin to beg God for forgiveness. "Oh, God, forgive me. Here I am praying and then I think such a terrible thought. What is wrong with me? I am such a terrible person."

Meanwhile, I've stopped praying and the enemy is gloating and saying to himself, "He's so easy."

> *But now you will know the truth, and the truth will set you free. Every now and then I'll have something like that happen and I'll just say, "You must take me for an idiot. I know where that's coming from. In Jesus' name, no." Then I keep right on with what I'm doing.*
>
> *The power of sin seeks to control us through our thoughts. Next time the power of sin rises up in your thoughts, renounce it. Make it Christ's prisoner. Take authority over that thought. The power of sin in your body is not who you are.*

Day Four

Today, we're going to come to the place where the Bible and your own personal experience come together. We're going to discuss the way to experience power over sin. What do you do when temptation rises up in your life? I certainly haven't suggested that Christians will reach a place of sinless perfection in this world. Let's face it, at times we will foolishly choose to act independently and sin.

What can you do when the power of sin exerts itself? How do you overcome sin? There are common ways you have probably tried to overcome temptation in your own life. Write the two most common below.

1. _____

2. _____

Here is where experiencing the grace walk makes all the difference in the world in your life. There are two practical principles we will consider today that will enable you to walk victoriously over temptation as you trust Jesus within you to enable you to practice them.

We Must Recognize Our Condition in Christ

Romans 6:1

To experience the grace walk when we are tempted, we need to understand our condition in Christ and how that affects our relationship to sin. Look again at Romans 6:1: "He who has died is freed from sin." We have studied this in a previous chapter, but this bears repeating so that you can see how it relates to temptation.

You have died to sin. You have been joined together with Jesus Christ on the cross, and the old you who loved to sin is dead. Sin has no power over you anymore. Any power that sin seems to have is just an illusion.

Have you ever noticed elephants at a circus? Outside the big tent, you may see a great big elephant shackled to an insignificant stake in the ground. The truth is, the elephant could walk away any time he wanted to go, but he doesn't. The stake holds him captive because he believes it can, so he never tries to walk away. He isn't held captive by the chain. He is held captive by the illusion. He believes a lie.

> *In reality, the chains of sin have been broken and you are free.*

Sin has no power over you, but if you don't believe that, you are in trouble. You may believe you are still held in bondage to sin. If so, you are believing a lie. That kind of negative faith will keep you in bondage to sins. In reality, the chains of sin have been broken and you are free.

In the space below, write a declaration of your faith that through the cross you have been set free from the power of sin over you. Be bold in your declaration, even if you don't feel it is true because your circumstances seem to indicate otherwise.

_____

_____

_____

_____

_____

So what are you to do when temptation comes? You are to respond, "I'm dead to sin! This temptation has no power over me. Lord Jesus, my life is in You. Now You express Your righteousness through me in the face of this temptation to do evil."

> *You are to respond, "I'm dead to sin! This temptation has no power over me. Lord Jesus, my life is in You. Now You express Your righteousness through me in the face of this temptation to do evil."*
>
> **Romans 8:2**

One man said that before he understood this, he used to hear temptation knock at the door. He would answer the door and say, "No, I can't go with you. I shouldn't because I'm a Christian." He said he often failed, giving in to the persuasive power of indwelling sin. "Now," he said, "when temptation comes knocking at my door, I simply say, 'Jesus, will you answer that?'" Do you see the difference? Christ within you will overcome temptation. You'll never do it by your own determination.

We Must Rest in Our Position in Christ

This principle is exciting because through it, you can enjoy freedom over sin like you have never known. Look at this verse carefully: "The law of the Spirit of life in Christ Jesus has set you free from the law of sin and of death" (Romans 8:2).

There are two laws mentioned in this verse. What are they?

1. The law of _____

2. The law of _____

To help make the promise in this verse applicable in your life, think of the law of sin and death functioning like the law of gravity. It is always at work trying to pull you down.

The law of sin and death is always present, seeking to pull the Christian down into independent living at every moment, but there is another law in which the Christian may rest. It is the law of the Spirit of life in Christ Jesus. Think of it functioning like the law of aerodynamics. The latter law will always supersede the former. As we trust Him, Jesus will never fail to overcome the law of sin and death.

Imagine you're told that a man jumped off the Empire State Building in New York City. What image comes to your mind? You may ask many questions about that incident, but one thing you would never ask is, "Did he fall?" You would assume the man fell because of your understanding of the law of gravity. It is a universal law which always exists.

"I wonder if he'll fall."

What if you were then told that the man who jumped was holding onto a hang glider? Your mental picture immediately changes because of another law—the law of aerodynamics. With the added information, you wouldn't envision the man falling, but instead you would imagine him soaring over the skyline of New York.

While you recognize the law of gravity, you also understand that, in a situation like this, the law of aerodynamics would overcome the law of gravity. Does the law of gravity cease to exist while the man is soaring on the hang glider? Not at all, but the man is resting in a higher law.

So it is with the believer. While the power of sin always resides within the Christian, the law of sin and death is not able to find its expression as long as the believer rests in the sufficiency of Christ.

At every moment that we depend totally on Him to express His life through us, we will experience victory over sin.

What would happen if the man in the hang glider decided he wanted to function independently of it? At the exact moment he decided to function independently, the law of gravity would once again become operative and he would immediately fall. If he chose to separate himself from the hang glider, nobody would be surprised that he fell. In fact, they wouldn't expect anything else.

When a Christian abides in Christ, depending on Him as his life source at every moment, he will experience victory over sin. However, at any moment a Christian decides to function apart from Jesus, he will sin. There is no other possibility for him. There is no middle ground. Either a person is choosing to depend entirely on Christ or else he is not. When your lifestyle is absorbed into your intimacy with Him, victory is the natural expression of His life within you. You can soar above the downward pull of indwelling sin because you are carried along by the gentle breeze of His love.

You will never be free from the presence of sin as long as you live in the physical body you now possess. But as you experience the grace walk, you will find freedom over the power of sin that resides in your body. Jesus Christ is the key to victory over temptation.

End your study time today by praying and acknowledging that you know you are dead to sin. Affirm that, at this very moment, you are trusting Jesus to express His life through you so you will be enabled to overcome the law of sin and death and walk in consistent victory.

You have learned this week why you commit sins. It is associated with the indwelling sin that is in your body. You aren't a bad person. You just haven't received your glorified body and must daily deal with that fact.

You have discovered that victory over temptation only comes through Christ as we recognize we are dead to sin. Then we must rest in the law of the Spirit of life in Christ Jesus, understanding that by Him we have *already* been given victory.

Today I want to share one final grace-principle that will revolutionize the way you face temptation and enable you to triumph over it. It has to do with what you spend your time thinking about, or where you set your mind. Here is the principle: Sooner or later, your actions will become an expression of your thoughts.

Many Christians spend a lot of time thinking about their sins, trying to figure out ways to overcome them. But victory will never come that way. Victory is a gift, given to us in Jesus Christ. You'll never experience victory by trying harder. It will only come by trusting Him.

If you want victory over sin, you must set your mind on Christ. It is impossible to overcome temptation by setting our mind on temptation. Set your mind on Jesus. If you set your mind on the sin, you'll never know victory.

To think that concentrating on overcoming our sins will give us victory is a totally wrong approach to the matter. Not only will setting our mind on the flesh fail to bring victory, it will actually perpetuate our defeat. Legalism will always focus on behavior, but when we are experiencing the grace walk we will focus on Jesus!

Romans 8:5-6

Those who are according to the flesh set their minds on the things of the flesh, but those who are according to the Spirit, the things of the Spirit. For the mind set on the flesh is death, but the mind set on the Spirit is life and peace (Romans 8:5-6).

If a person sets his mind on the things of the flesh, what does it produce?

_____

_____

If you set your mind on the things of the Spirit, what will be the result?

_____

_____

If you set your mind on the sins of the flesh, it should come as no surprise when your behavior matches your mind-set. That is bound to happen sooner or later. You guarantee your own failure when you decide to overcome sin by concentrating on it. It will make no difference that you ask God to help you.

God won't bless our efforts to deliver ourselves from sin after we have been saved any more than He would help us overcome sin before we were saved. He wants to use our futile attempts to achieve victory over sin through our own efforts to force our attention toward Jesus. As long as we try to gain victory through our behavior, He will patiently wait until we have exhausted all our efforts, then He will do for us what we can't do for ourselves. It is at that point we are ready to receive His answer.

When I was a teen, I loved to play basketball. Every single day I couldn't wait to get home from school so I could rush out into the backyard to play ball. We would play until dark every day. Fridays were especially exciting because we didn't have school the next day. Our parents would often allow us to stay out really late, shooting baskets when we could hardly even see the goal. It was an adolescent boy's paradise.

One Sunday when I was barely 16 years old our family went to church. While sitting in the Sunday school class that morning, I noticed a new girl who walked into the class. I had never seen her before. I had never been on a date up to that time. When this girl walked past me, I checked her out—I mean, I *discerned* that this might be a good place to begin my dating life. I went home and asked my dad the big question. "Dad, if I get a date some Friday night, will you let me use your car to go out?"

"Do you have a date?" my dad asked, probably glad to see his only son moving toward manhood.

"Not yet, but there's a girl I want to go out with if you'll let me have the car," I answered.

"Who is she?" he asked.

"Just a girl I met at church last week," I answered.

"Okay," he said. "You can use the car if you get a date."

I couldn't wait until the next Sunday. As soon as church was over I made a beeline for this new, good-looking girl. After nervous small talk, I took the plunge. "Are you doing anything this Friday night?" I asked. "No," she answered, "why?" "Well, there's a new Barbra

Streisand movie coming out this weekend. I thought we would go see it and then go over to Pizza Villa after the movie, if you want to," I said. "Sure, that sounds like fun," she answered.

The following Friday night I picked her up and went out on my first date. It went really well. The next day my buddies all rushed over to my house bright and early. "Man, where were you?" they demanded to know. "We waited for you to come out. We play basketball *every* Friday!" they continued with obvious irritation over my reckless disregard for our sacred appointed game. "What were you doing?" Holding my shoulders back and my head high, I answered, "Boys, I was on a date!"

To their dismay, I called the girl and asked her to go out with me the following Friday. She accepted. In fact, I went out with her every Friday for the next three years, then I married her. We've been married since 1973. Now that I think about it, I can't remember the last time I played basketball on Friday night. I've found something better!

If somebody had told me that at age 16 I would have to give up Friday-night basketball, I would have rebelled against the very thought of such a thing. As it turned out, I didn't focus on giving it up. I simply became obsessed with something I wanted more than those things. You could say that Melanie delivered me from Friday-night basketball. It wasn't a struggle for me. I just set my mind on her, and basketball sort of faded away.

That's how Jesus can deliver us from our sins! When we come to know who Jesus is in us and who we are in Him, we discover that sins we once couldn't imagine living without lose their appeal to us. We don't experience victory by struggling against sins, but by setting our mind on Jesus. The apostle Paul said it succinctly in Colossians 3:1-3:

> *If you have been raised up with Christ, keep seeking the things above, where Christ is, seated at the right hand of God. Set your mind on things above, not on the things that are on earth. For you have died and your life is hidden with Christ in God.*

Colossians 3:1-3

We will never overcome sin through sheer determination and self-discipline. That kind of negative motivation keeps our eyes off Jesus and on our sins. We are to focus on Him, not sin! As we fall more and more in love with Jesus, those sins we have so tightly embraced will become increasingly unattractive to us until we *want* to let them go.

As you end this week of study, read the following verses and underline the phrases that tell you anything about victory. Underneath each verse, summarize what you learn about victory from that statement.

> *Thanks be to God, who always leads us in triumph in Christ, and manifests through us the sweet aroma of the knowledge of Him in every place (2 Corinthians 2:14).*

2 Corinthians 2:14

Summarize the truth about victory:

_____

_____

> *Thanks be to God, who gives us the victory through our Lord Jesus Christ (1 Corinthians 15:57).*

1 Corinthians 15:57

Summarize the truth about victory:

_____

_____

Romans 8:37

In all these things we overwhelmingly conquer through Him who loved us (Romans 8:37).

Summarize the truth about victory:

_____

_____

The cause of sin in your life as a Christian stems from indwelling sin. The cure is the indwelling life of Jesus Christ, who lives inside you. Appropriate the truths you have studied this week, and you will see a tremendous difference in your life.

TRYING TO LIVE
BY RELIGIOUS RULES
IS THE SUREST WAY
TO LIVE DEFEATED

In the past five weeks you have learned life-changing truths that will enable you to experience the grace walk. You've seen that it isn't by your trying, but instead by your *dying* with Jesus Christ, that your old sin nature was put to death and you received His holy nature. You have learned that victory over temptation doesn't come by struggling against it, but rather by resting in Him as your victory.

Day One

This week we are going to examine a very practical part of the Christian walk. It has to do with your relationship to religious rules. Trying to live by religious rules is the surest way to experience defeat. Sometimes those who, like me, were reared in an environment that stressed the importance of keeping the rules struggle with this concept.

For that reason, I want to bring you back again to a foundational question I have kept in front of you all along: Do you believe the Bible? Is it your final authority? As you study this week, compare what you read in this study with what the Bible says—and if you see that Scripture says something different from what you've always believed, then give up your old viewpoint. Accept what the Bible says, whatever that may be.

Married to the Law

Let's begin this study on our relationship to rules by examining what the Bible teaches about our relationship to the law before coming to know Christ. Scripture teaches that before we came to know Jesus Christ, we came into this world married to the law.

Using the metaphor of marriage isn't something I created. It is the one Paul uses in the passage of Scripture we're going to focus on today. When did we get married to the law? It happened in the Garden of Eden, when Adam ate from the law tree. It was at that moment he became joined in union to the law.

When Adam married the law, all of mankind became united to the law in the same way. Consequently, we are all born into the world under a system of religious legalism. We are all natural-born legalists. The default setting for mankind's guidelines for behavior revolve around issues of morality—right vs. wrong.

To apply that concept to our spiritual lives is not God's intent. Our relationship to Him doesn't rest on what we do, right or wrong. Instead it is grounded in Jesus Christ. Legalism is all about what we do, but the heart of grace revolves around what Jesus has already done.

Here is a working definition for legalism. It might be helpful to you to memorize it: *Legalism is a system of living in which we try to make spiritual progress or gain God's blessings based on what we do.* On the other hand, grace is a system of living in which God blesses us because we're in Jesus Christ, and for no other reason.

Living by the law finds its roots in *our* actions, not God's. This fact can be seen in Exodus 19:5. Moses came down from the mountain and read God's law to the Israelites. God told them, "*If* you will obey Me and keep My covenant, *then* you will be My special people." The law was filled with "if-then" statements: "If you do so and so, then I'll bless you."

> *Legalism is a system of living in which we try to make spiritual progress or gain God's blessings based on what we do.*

Exodus 19:5

Deuteronomy 28:15

Later in the Old Testament (Deuteronomy 28:15), God added that if His people failed to do those things He commanded, all kinds of curses would come upon them. So the law says that we will be blessed if we do certain things and cursed if we fail to do them. Do right and be blessed, do wrong and be cursed—that's the bottom line with the law. Considering that we are all born married to the law, that is hardly an encouraging system for anybody.

Romans 7:1-5

Consider what Paul said about our marriage to the law in Romans 7:1-5.

Do you not know, brethren (for I am speaking to those who know the law), that the law has jurisdiction over a person as long as he lives? For the married woman is bound by law to her husband while he is living; but if her husband dies, she is released from the law concerning the husband. So then, if while her husband is living she is joined to another man, she shall be called an adulteress; but if her husband dies, she is free from the law, so that she is not an adulteress though she is joined to another man.

Therefore, my brethren, you also were made to die to the Law through the body of Christ, so that you might be joined to another, to Him who was raised from the dead, in order that we might bear fruit for God. For while we were in the flesh, the sinful passions, which were aroused by the Law, were at work in the members of our body to bear fruit for death.

Based on this passage from the book of Romans, answer the following questions:

How long does the relationship last between the law and somebody born into this world?

_____

Using the example of laws governing marriage, how can a person become free from the law?

_____

The Bible teaches that there is only one way out of the relationship we have with the law when we come into this world. That way is by death. Marriage is " 'til death do us part."

Later in the week, we will look more closely at this idea of being free from the law through death. For now, answer the following questions based on the content of the Bible passage you have just read.

In the marriage between a person and the law, which partner dies?

_____

How does that partner die?

_____

> As you end your study today, think about the definition already given for the law. Pray and ask the Holy Spirit to show you ways you may still be living as a legalist and not completely walking in grace.

Yesterday you learned that we are all born as legalists because of Adam's choice to eat from the law tree in the garden of Eden. Today I want you to ask the Holy Spirit to show you the extent to which you might still be trying to live by law. We are going to look at two characteristics of a person who is living by the law. Check the box beside the statements which apply to you.

☐ **1. Legalistic Christians constantly battle feelings of self-condemnation.**

When we relate to Mr. Law, we will discover he is always condemning, always critical, always pointing out our failures and our faults. A person who is involved with the law will always be keenly aware of personal shortcomings. Mr. Law is always telling you, "You're wrong! Shame on you! You're wrong! You're wrong! You're wrong!"

2 Corinthians 3:7

2 Corinthians 3:9

Paul calls the law "the ministry of death" in 2 Corinthians 3:7. Then in 2 Corinthians 3:9 he calls the law "the ministry of condemnation." You just can't please Mr. Law no matter how hard you try. He points out every detail of how you've missed the mark. He is never satisfied. If you excel in one area, he'll point out another area where you're failing.

Consider your own life. Have you tried to build your life around religious rules as a means for making spiritual progress? If so, make no mistake about it, the law has ministered death to you in some way. It might have been the death of your joy. Rules may have killed your peace. Think about your life, and identify at least two ways that trying to live by rules has ministered a sense of death and condemnation to you.

1. _____

_____

2. _____

_____

Do you see the problem? Living as a legalist will never bring a sense of contentment to us about our spiritual condition. The one word Mr. Law will never say is "enough." He'll always demand more and more and more. Trying to live by rules will create in us a constant sense of failure and frustration. We will experience feelings of spiritual inferiority and self-condemnation because we aren't doing better.

Yet, despite all this pointing out of failure, Mr. Law never helps us become godly. He'll tell you everything you're doing wrong, but he won't lift a finger to help you. In fact, his influence will cause just the opposite result.

2. Legalistic Christians constantly struggle with sin.

It would seem that a person who builds his life around moral rules of behavior would live a consistently victorious life, but it doesn't work that way. Rules can never produce holiness in your lifestyle. "If a law had been given which was able to impart life, then righteousness would indeed have been based on the law" (Galatians 3:21).

Galatians 3:21

Romans 7:5

Not only will law not enable you to live a godly lifestyle, it will actually stir up and activate sin in your life. Look again at Romans 7. Verse 5 says, "While we were in the flesh, the sinful passions, which were *aroused by the Law,* were at work in the members of our body to bear fruit for death." What does Paul say arouses sinful passions? The law.

Romans 7:8

For many years, I thought that embracing religious rules would control my sinful passions, but the Scripture says just the opposite. The law *stirs up* sinful passions. In Romans 7:8 the Bible says, "Sin, taking opportunity through the commandment, produced in me coveting of every kind; for apart from the Law sin is dead."

The word *opportunity* is the Greek word *aphorme*. A Greek lexicon defines the word as "a place from which a movement or attack is made; a base of operation." Take the meaning of that word in the verse above and describe in your own words the link between the law (religious rules) and the act of committing a sin.

_____

_____

_____

Romans 7:5

Have you thought that if you built your life around the right list of religious rules it would keep you from sinning? What you're really doing is *fertilizing* sin. Remember that Romans 7:5 says that "sinful passions are aroused by the law."

Do you see this principle at work in your life in any area? Do you notice that the sin you most want to be free from seems to have the strongest hold in your life? Write out your observations based on the new concepts of grace and law. How have rules affected the level of victory you have known in your life?

Consider what the Bible says in 1 Corinthians 15:56: "The power of sin is the law." The law (religious rules) is to sin what gasoline is to a car's engine. Rules fuel sin.

1 Corinthians 15:56

For instance, do you remember how easy it was to read your Bible when you first became a Christian? You didn't read it because you ought to, but because you wanted to read God's Word. Then, somewhere along the way, you were told that you *ought* to read the Bible every day. Bible reading then became a rule, a law, to you.

What effect did that have in your life? Didn't you find that when reading the Bible became your duty, it became hard to make yourself consistently read it? That's what the Law will always do to a person.

End today's study by reflecting on the rules you have tried to use to make progress spiritually. They have either caused you to feel condemned or spiritually proud. Are you beginning to see that the Christian life isn't intended to be built around rules? Christianity is a relationship.

Romans 9:30-32

Today we will focus on another aspect of a legalistic Christian life built around rules. Legalistic Christians try to make spiritual progress through their actions. They believe that if they just do the right things consistently, they will advance spiritually and become more righteous. Have you fallen victim to this lie? Consider Romans 9:30-32. It makes the lie very obvious.

What shall we say then? That Gentiles, who did not pursue righteousness, attained righteousness, even the righteousness which is by faith; but Israel, pursuing a law of righteousness, did not arrive at that law. Why? Because they did not pursue it by faith, but as though it were by works. They stumbled over the stumbling stone.

These Jews were like many Christians today. Imagine them trying, working hard to achieve righteousness. They always keep the law in mind. Step by step, they try to advance by obeying the law. Their actions say, "Step one: We have to remember the Sabbath Day to keep it holy. Step two: We have to honor our father and mother. Step three: Do not steal. Step four: Do not commit adultery." On and on goes the list.

They are intent on keeping the law and becoming righteous. Then Jesus comes on the scene and He says, "Do you want to be righteous? I'm your righteousness. Trust Me." These Jews respond, "Get out of our way! Can't You see what we are doing here?" And on they go, focusing on the law, trying to achieve righteousness.

Meanwhile, the Gentiles are watching this. They see the Jews living a rigorous lifestyle. They see how hard they are working to live pure lives, following all the rules. The Gentiles could have remarked,

"There's no way we could ever do that! We could never live up to that kind of lifestyle. It would take a miracle for us to become righteous!"

God hears them and responds, "Exactly. You could never do it. You could never achieve it. You'll just have to receive it." So the Jews who were trying so hard to become righteous never became righteous. But the Gentiles, who didn't even try, just received it as a gift.

Can you see how these Jews were acting like many Christians today? Many are still living with that Old Covenant mentality. They're trying to become righteous by following religious rules. They think they will achieve righteousness by taking those actions. But the truth is, none of those things will cause you to achieve righteousness. Spiritual growth comes by ongoing faith in Jesus. It doesn't happen by attempting to achieve it through our own behavior.

> *Spiritual growth comes by ongoing faith in Jesus.*

Those things that you are trying to do in order to become more righteous will never help you reach your goal. The actions of the Christian life are intended to be the overflow of the righteousness of Christ, which is *already in you*.

Since rules stimulate us to sin, what is the believer to do with the commandments of the New Testament? You may be thinking, *But doesn't behavior matter? Didn't Jesus say that if we love Him, we will keep His commandments?* (see John 14:15). He did indeed. Yet when grace rules a person's life, he will approach the commandments of the New Testament with a totally different attitude than the legalist.

John 14:15

> **Obedience is the natural response of the Christian who loves Jesus.**

Legalism presents the commandments as divine ultimatums coming from a harsh Judge. When law rules a person, the tone of the words of Jesus are heard like this: "If you love me, prove it by keeping my commandments."

A grace walk causes the Christian to approach the commandments with eager anticipation, not with fear and intimidation. This believer *understands* the words of Jesus when he said, "If you love me, you will keep my commandments." When we love Jesus, we *will* keep His commandments. Obedience is the natural response of the Christian who loves Jesus. Without love, the only thing we have to offer is lifeless compliance. Love is the basis for our obedience, not laws.

1 John 5:3

John stressed the relationship between love and our obedience to God's commandments when he said, "This is the love of God, that we keep His commandments; and His commandments are not burdensome" (1 John 5:3). It's not a strain for a Christian who is walking in grace to obey the commandments of God. It is a pleasure to be obedient!

Many who have understood the role of faith in salvation have lost sight of it when it comes to living the Christian life. They understood there was nothing they could do to save themselves, but now believe that somehow living the Christian life depends on them and how well they keep the rules. Paul said, "As you have received the Lord Jesus Christ, so walk ye in Him." You received Him by grace through faith. That's the way we are to walk.

In a healthy marriage, what is the motivation for keeping our marriage vows?

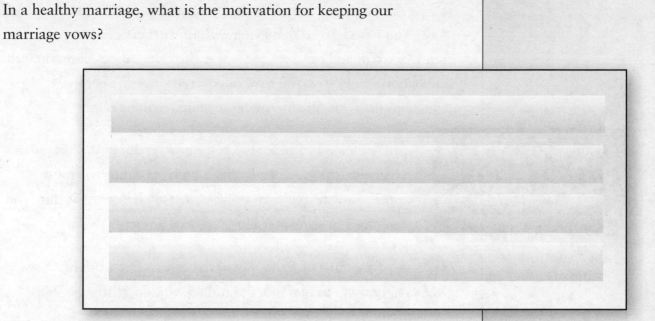

The same is true in our relationship to Jesus Christ. It isn't laws, but love that motivates us toward a godly lifestyle. We honor Him with our behavior because we love Him, not because of demands placed on us.

So far this week you have seen that you were born married to Mr. Law. You have learned that living with him produces an internal sense of death and condemnation over the fact you can never do well enough to satisfy law. You have discovered you can't become more righteous than you already are by keeping religious rules.

Romans 7:4

Today I want you to see the best news yet about the law. To experience the grace walk, this is a pivotal truth you must appropriate in your own walk with Jesus. The truth is this: You don't have any relationship to the law anymore. None.

Because of the cross of Jesus, you have been set free from Mr. Law. Your relationship to him is over, finished. Consider Romans 7:4:

> *My brethren, you also were made to die to the Law through the body of Christ, so that you might be joined to another, to Him who was raised from the dead, in order that we might bear fruit for God.*

Remember that we were all married to Mr. Law and marriage is "'til death do us part." That fact left us in a mess because Mr. Law is never going to die. God's law is eternal. So to get you out of the relationship you had to religious rules, God said, "Here's what I'll do. The Law is never going to die, but I'll let *you* die."

So that's exactly what happened. You died and, when you did, you were released from the law and its system of rules. You died and were born again, this time married to Mr. Grace. Read Romans 7:4 again slowly and meditate on what it is saying to you.

Believers have no relationship to the law anymore. Do you know what your relationship is to religious rules? You're dead to them. Where is the person who used to be married to the law? That person was crucified with Christ and is dead. Galatians 3:13 says that Christ redeemed (freed) us from the law. If it were necessary to still try to keep the law, then you wouldn't be redeemed from it. But the Bible says you *have* been redeemed from the law.

Your relationship to religious rules has ended. Some have suggested that Christians aren't under the law because the law died. However, it wasn't the law that died. It was *you* that died, with Christ on the cross. Mr. Law is still alive, but he is no longer married to those of us who are Christians.

Read 1 Timothy 1:8-11, then answer the questions that follow.

> *We know that the Law is good, if one uses it lawfully, realizing the fact that law is not made for a righteous person, but for those who are lawless and rebellious, for the ungodly and sinners, for the unholy and profane, for those who kill their fathers or mothers, for murderers and immoral men and homosexuals and kidnappers and liars and perjurers, and whatever else is contrary to sound teaching, according to the glorious gospel of the blessed God, with which I have been entrusted.*

Is the law good or bad?

_____

Is the law made for those who are righteous?

_____

Galatians 3:13

> *Believers have no relationship to the law anymore.*

1 Timothy 1:8-11

Are you righteous?

_____

The Purpose of the Law

Don't get the impression that the law is a bad thing. Paul said that the law is good if it is understood properly. What is the purpose of the law? It serves several good purposes:

1. The law stimulates sin in the lives of unbelievers. Romans 5:20 teaches that God brought His law into the world so sins might increase. Many people think the law was given to *decrease* sins, but that isn't what the Bible says. Why would God give the law to increase sins? It was so that sin might become exceedingly sinful. (Read Romans 7:13 in your Bible.) The law stimulates sins in self-righteous man, who thinks that he "isn't *that* bad."

Most unbelievers think that in the end their good works and bad works will be weighed. They mistakenly think that if their good deeds outweigh the bad ones, they will be granted entrance to heaven. The law destroys that kind of foolish thinking by exposing the sinfulness of man's heart.

2. The law is given to direct unbelievers to Christ. Galatians 3:24 teaches that the law is a tutor that leads people to Christ. In wealthy Greek and Roman families of Bible times, a tutor held the responsibility of seeing that children from age six to sixteen were delivered to the teacher for class every day. That is what the law does in the life of an

> **1. The law stimulates sin in the lives of unbelievers.**

Romans 5:20

Romans 7:13

> **2. The law is given to direct unbelievers to Christ.**

Galatians 3:24

unbeliever. It ministers condemnation to those outside Christ, and thereby drives them toward Him.

Once the tutor delivered his student to the teacher, his job was done. Galatians 3:25 says that when we become a Christian, "we are no longer under a tutor." Once you came to Christ, you didn't need the law anymore. You have Jesus now.

Galatians 3:25

As you conclude your study today, review what you have learned by answering the following questions:

How did you get out of the relationship you had to the law?

What are two purposes for the law?

The law will have the same effect on you now as it did before you became a Christian. What effect will trying to keep rules have on your ability to say no to sins?

Why don't Christians need the law anymore?

Matthew 11:28-29

Romans 8:1

Ephesians 1:6

At this point in your study, you should see that you are no longer under the law. You don't need rules to guide your life. You have the Holy Spirit living inside you, and He is capable of doing that. Once you came to Christ, the law completed its purpose in you. Now you are married to Mr. Grace—Jesus. This life is very different from your old life.

When you were married to Mr. Law you could never do enough to please him, but it's different being married to Mr. Grace. He offers a life of rest. Here's what He says:

Come to Me, all who are weary and heavy-laden, and I will give you rest. Take My yoke upon you and learn from Me, for I am gentle and humble in heart, and you will find rest for your souls. For My yoke is easy and My burden is light (Matthew 11:28-29).

If you had asked me before 1990 to describe my Christian experience, I never would have used words like "rest," and "easy," and "light." Religious legalism will drive you into the ground and keep demanding more. But the voice of Grace says, "Come to Me. I'll give you rest. You'll find rest for your soul." Before I learned these truths, I didn't know rest could be a gift. I thought it was a sin. Now I find out it's a gift from Jesus!

Being married to Jesus Christ is wonderful. He never condemns you (see Romans 8:1). He loves you passionately just the way you are and completely accepts you (see Ephesians 1:6).

Remember, you have no relationship to Mr. Law anymore. He is alive and well, but he's not married to you. You are now married to Jesus.

When you became a Christian, you received a new spirit, but you still have the same brain. You didn't get a brain transplant. Your brain remembers what it was like being married to Mr. Law. It is because of this fact that Christians often stumble back into a legalistic lifestyle.

If you're not careful, you may find yourself trying to relate to Jesus the way you used to relate to Mr. Law. It sometimes happens like this. The Christian asks, "Jesus, what do You want me to do for You? I'm so happy to be joined in marriage to You."

> Jesus:
> "I want you to just rest in Me and receive My love."

Jesus answers, "I want you to receive My love."

Christian: "Yes, Lord. Thank You so much for Your love. What do You want me to do for You now?"

Jesus: "I just want You to receive My love."

Christian: "Yes, Lord, I know You love me, but what do You want me to do for You? What can I *do* for You?"

Jesus: "I want you to just rest in Me and receive My love."

For the Christian who doesn't know his identity, this can become frustrating. He doesn't know what God knows—that if he'll just rest and receive the love of Jesus, everything else will flow out of that love.

When we don't know our identity in Christ, if we don't know what it means to simply rest in His love, we may get frustrated and take our eyes off Jesus. We start looking around. Guess who shows up at that moment—Mr. Law. He is always on the prowl, looking for vulnerable Christians who don't know their identity.

If you don't walk in your true identity, you then may make eye contact with Mr. Law, who asks, "May I help you?"

"Well, can *you* tell me what I'm supposed to do?"

"At your service," says Mr. Law. He steps right up and gives you all the religious rules you want. Before you know it, you find yourself in a situation where you are married to Mr. Grace, but you're involved with Mr. Law. Your lifestyle is built around rules again.

What is it called when somebody is married to one person, but involved with another?

_____

_____

Romans 7:1-5

Spiritual adultery exists when you build your life around rules. Do you see it in Romans 7? The first five verses here are teaching us about our relationship to the law. We were married to the law, but we died to the law in the body of Christ and now we're married to Jesus. Paul says that if you are married to one person but get involved with another, you are committing adultery. When you are married to Jesus but involved with the law, you are committing adultery.

Are you involved in spiritual adultery? Break off your relationship with religious rules! So many of us have been enticed away from Jesus to have an affair with another. Jesus wants our complete love and devotion.

Titus 2:11-12

Some people are afraid of this freedom. They mistakenly think this kind of unlimited grace may encourage sin, but it doesn't. Titus 2:11-12 explains:

> *The grace of God has appeared, bringing salvation to all men, instructing us to deny ungodliness and worldly desires and to live sensibly, righteously and godly in the present age.*

Does grace teach you to sin? No. Grace teaches us to say *no* to sin by changing our very nature.

Grace motivates us toward obedience through our love and desire for Jesus Christ. There was a time before we were saved when we had no inner desire to live a godly lifestyle. "But now we have been released from the Law, having died to that by which we were bound, so that we serve in newness of the Spirit and not in oldness of the letter" (Romans 7:6). In this newness of the Spirit, we remind ourselves that we died to the law and are no longer obligated to religious rules. Finally we are free to serve God because we *want* to, not because we *have* to. Legalists aren't free to serve the Lord, they are obligated to do it.

Romans 7:6

Don't be afraid of the freedom grace offers. You have the Holy Spirit living inside you. He will ensure that your daily walk is an expression of your relationship to Christ if you will just trust Him.

> Don't be afraid of the freedom grace offers.

Review these concepts, noticing how your understanding is increasing.

What effect does legalism have on a believer's life?

What effect does grace have in a believer's life?

Why don't you need to build your life around religious rules anymore?

How will it affect your life if you do try to live by rules instead of out of your relationship to Jesus?

GOD MAY BE TOTALLY DIFFERENT FROM HOW YOU HAVE IMAGINED HIM TO BE

Day One

We have been looking at central truths about life in Jesus Christ. Each week of your study, you have learned a new key to experiencing the grace walk. We have discussed the fact that many of us aren't experiencing victory because we are trying too hard. Does it seem strange that *trying* to experience a victorious Christian life would be the very cause for your not experiencing victory? The fact is, we don't gain victory by our self-effort. Victory is a gift.

Here's some news that can change you: This life we have in Christ is not about you. It's about Him. It's about Jesus Christ—Jesus, who loves you so much that He gave Himself *for you* so He could give Himself *to you* and live His life *through you*.

We are building an understanding of how to gain victory over the power of sin by simply allowing Jesus to live His life through us. Victory isn't up to you. It's up to Him. In this lesson, we will begin to address some very practical aspects of experiencing His life and the victory the Bible promises.

I will address two specific areas of experiencing the grace walk that I think are essential and need to be examined in the modern church. Many people, it seems to me, are snared by misunderstanding in these two areas.

Our Concept of God

The first area I want to talk to you about is our concept of God. If we're going to fully experience the life of Jesus Christ, we must have a solid understanding of the personality of God. I want to ask you this question: What if God is nothing like you imagine Him to be? Having seen a broad spectrum of the body of Christ, I can tell you that for much of the modern church, this is the case. God may be nothing like we have imagined Him to be. Some of us have built a caricature of God in our minds that is not in line with the God we see described in the Bible and revealed in Jesus Christ.

Pause here for a moment and write a short description of how you would describe God based on how you have come to know Him. Don't write a "churchy" description based on what you think you ought to say. Instead, describe God based on the honest perception you have come to have of Him based on your own experience.

_____

_____

_____

_____

Some of us have an imaginary character in our minds that is a long way from what the Bible tells us about the God who is our Father. Many people have false concepts of God. Over the next few days, I want to address several of those faulty beliefs.

The first faulty concept of God is that many people perceive Him like a Divine Employer

Some see God as if He's the Boss and they're the employee. Their understanding of their relationship to God is that He is a master and the believer is a slave. Their focus is only on His lordship.

It is true that God is Lord and Master, but He is more than that. I taught for many years that Jesus Christ wants to be your Savior, but if you want to go all the way in your walk of faith, you have to acknowledge Him as your Lord. While that's not untrue, it doesn't tell the whole story.

> **The greatest calling of Scripture is... to understand that He is our very life.**

I used to think that the pinnacle of success in the Christian life was to relate to Jesus as Lord. I would often teach, "Jesus wants to be Lord over every area of your life." But now I realize that making that statement puts us on shaky ground. We've already learned that you don't have a life apart from Jesus Christ. He doesn't want to be Lord over every area of *your* life. Any life you possess is *His* life. I've come to believe that the greatest calling of Scripture is not just to know Him as Savior, not just to know Him as Lord, but to understand that *He is our very life.*

Look at the following words of Jesus. Let Him speak them right to your heart. Really hear what He is saying to you.

> *You are My friends if you do what I command you. No longer do I call you slaves, for the slave does not know what his master is doing; but I have called you friends, for all things that I have heard from My Father I have made known to you (John 15:14-15).*

John 15:14-15

Why does He not call you a slave?

_____

What is Jesus making known to you?

_____

_____

So many Christians, though genuinely born again, are living under the law by trying to make Jesus become their Lord. He is more than Lord. He is *life*. There are many who, after being saved, have gradually drifted into empty religion. They have lost their focus on their relationship to Christ and aren't experiencing any joy in their walk.

Christianity and the Christian religion are worlds apart. In fact, the Christian religion is no better than any other religion in the world. It isn't religion that Christ came to offer. He came to give us Himself. That which causes Christianity to be real and to be alive is the living Jesus. Without Him, it stops being Christianity and becomes nothing more than another dead religion.

> *Christianity and the Christian religion are worlds apart.*

Many Christians believe that God is our divine employer and as we make Him Lord by doing what He says, then He's fine with us. That falls so far short of what the Bible teaches. In Galatians 4:4-7 Paul says that we are no longer slaves, but sons. Look carefully at that passage and answer the questions that follow.

Galatians 4:4-7

> *When the fullness of the time came, God sent forth His Son, born of a woman, born under the Law, so that He might redeem those who were under the Law, that we might receive the adoption as sons. Because you are sons, God has sent forth the Spirit of His Son into our hearts, crying, "Abba! Father!" Therefore you are no longer a slave, but a son; and if a son, then an heir through God.*

Circle the phrase "so that." It implies cause and effect, or an action and its result. What is the action and the result connected by this phrase?

_____

_____

Circle the next occurrence of "that." What action caused what result?

_____

_____

The chain of events so far is 1) God sent forth His Son, *so that* 2) He might redeem me, *so that* 3) I would be adopted as a son. Now, circle the word "because." It implies a link between two circumstances. What does the "because" link?

Because I am adopted as a son, He puts the life of the Son in me. Circle the word "therefore." It implies a direct cause and effect. What thoughts does the word "therefore" connect?

Because I am a son, *therefore* I cannot be a slave.

You're not just a slave anymore. You're more than that. You're a son. The attitude of an employee is likely to be, "How little can I do and still keep the boss happy?" But the son knows he is an heir to the business. He doesn't have to keep asking the boss what to do or what not to do. He has the same dream, the same vision as his father. He has absorbed the mind of his dad. He's a partner in the business with his dad.

So many of us go through our Christian life saying to God, "Tell me what I'm supposed to do and I'll do it. What do you want me to do? That's what I'll do." That is a legalistic perspective. You aren't a slave. You are a joint-heir with Jesus.

In Exodus 21:1-6 you will find the ordinances about slavery.

Exodus 21:1-6

These are the ordinances which you are to set before them: If you buy a Hebrew slave, he shall serve for six years; but on the seventh he shall go out as a free man without payment. If he comes alone, he shall go out alone; if he is the husband of a wife, then his wife shall go out with him. If his master gives him a wife, and she bears him sons or daughters, the wife and her children shall belong to her master, and he shall go out alone. But if the slave plainly says, "I love my master, my wife and my children; I will not go out as a free man," then his master shall bring him to God, then he shall bring him to the door or the doorpost. And his master shall pierce his ear with an awl; and he shall serve him permanently.

This is the picture of a man who says, "I love my master. I want to be a servant." Yes, we are servants. We're servants because we want to be, because we love Him and want to serve Him. We're sons who have chosen to be servants of Jesus Christ.

Yesterday you learned you aren't just God's servant. You are His child. Today we are going to consider another faulty concept of God that will interfere with your experiencing the grace walk.

A second faulty perception of God is that He is a harsh judge

Day Two

Many people picture God sitting in heaven, scrutinizing every act, watching, waiting for them to make a mistake. They picture God with a frown on His face. "What are you doing now?" they hear Him saying. In their minds, He's always in a bad mood. They see Him as an impatient parent who's ready to spank the child who's getting on his nerves. Punitive. Harsh. Judgmental. Critical.

Romans 8:1

That's not how it is with your heavenly Father. Your heavenly Father never condemns you. Romans 8:1 says, "There is now *no condemnation* for those who are in Christ Jesus." No condemnation. God does not condemn you. If you envision God as a harsh judge, it will be hard to experience intimacy with Him. It's hard to warm up to someone who you think doesn't like you. Haven't you found that to be true?

Maybe, like many people, you believe God doesn't really like you. Oh, you know He loves you. He has to love you. After all, He's God and that goes with the job description. But to like you? If you believe God doesn't like you, you will find it hard to understand the intimacy and the joy you could have in relationship to Him, because you have a false understanding of His attitude toward you.

Do you recognize subtle misconceptions about God in your thinking? List them.

_____

_____

_____

_____

Now, beside each misconception, write the truth and cross out the lie.

The third misunderstanding about God is that He is a distant deity

Some see God as big and sovereign—and He is those things. But they see Him as removed from them. To them, He is "out there." They imagine a majestic deity who doesn't have time for or interest in their petty circumstances. They imagine He saved them and will one day take them to heaven, but in the meantime, they must do their best.

This view of God resembles deism. It suggests that God created us and wound us up, and has now stepped back and is letting us run our course. Those with this viewpoint see God as if He were a distant deity, not involved in the details of our lives.

Nothing could be further from the truth. Ephesians 2:13 tells us,

> _Now in Christ Jesus you who formerly were far off have been brought near by the blood of Christ._

God is up close and personal in your life.

Ephesians 2:13

God is up close and personal in your life. You aren't just *close* to God, you're *one with Him* through Christ. He's not in some distant place looking down, watching those He loves as if we were ants scurrying around. He doesn't see you as part of a mass multitude.

I've heard people say, "When I pray, I don't bother God with the little things. He has so many bigger things going on that are more important than my little issues. I'm just not going to bother Him with the small stuff."

> ### When He looks at you, He looks at you with delight.

Let me remind you, to Him it's all small stuff. You won't wear Him out. You won't bother Him. He's not a distant deity who is unconcerned and uninvolved in the details of your life.

What Is God Really Like?

How can we know what God is like? We know by what the Bible tells us. One thing the Bible tells us about God is that He is loving and laughing. Can you imagine a happy God? That's who He is. He's a happy God. He's in a good mood. Always.

The cross of Jesus Christ and the empty tomb have put a smile on God's face that nothing will wipe off. When He looks at you, He looks at you with delight.

Zephaniah 3:17

Look at Zephaniah 3:17.

> *The LORD your God is in your midst,*
> *A victorious warrior.*
> *He will exult over you with joy,*
> *He will be quiet in His love,*
> *He will rejoice over you with shouts of joy.*

Notice the extravagant language of this verse, describing a God who is celebrating with enthusiasm. He looks at you and becomes excited with joy. He adores you!

Stop reading for a moment and try this experiment. Be still and quiet. Let the reality of the scene described in Zephaniah 3:17 (with *you* in it) play out in your imagination. Imagine this—God is *exulting* over you. The word means to twirl, to dance with enthusiasm. He rejoices over you with shouts of joy. Can you imagine such a thing?

Picture it like this. God looks at you and His heart swells with pride and love. He begins to shout out in the heavens, "Come here! Look at my child! Gather around, everybody! I am so proud! Isn't this person just beautiful? Oh, you should have seen how she started out. What a mess. I had to kill that old person and start all over. But look at her now. Is she a work of art or not? I am so excited about her."

> *God looks at you and His heart swells with pride and love. ..."I am so excited about her."*

Zephaniah 3:17

This scenario is consistent with what Scripture teaches. The Bible says that in the ages to come God will show the exceeding riches of His grace *in us*. That's not a matter of pretending. That's exactly how He's looking at you. He's loving and laughing.

We are the bride of Christ. One day He's going to bring us home and we're going to start our eternal honeymoon with Him. I've never seen a bridegroom yet who is not madly in love with his fiancée and anxious to be with her. He adores you.

End your study time today quietly meditating on the love God has for you. Renounce the faulty concepts you have had concerning who He is and affirm His true personality in your mind. Ask the Holy

Spirit to renew your mind to the truth of His passionate love for you. Then write a declaration of His love for you in the space below.

_____

_____

_____

_____

_____

_____

*The **LORD** your God is in your midst,*
A victorious warrior.
He will exult over you with joy,
He will be quiet in His love,
He will rejoice over you with shouts of joy.

—Zephaniah 3:17

_____

_____

_____

_____

It is important to realize that God doesn't just love you, He *likes* you. Many Christians believe God loves them, but it's better than that. God actually likes you. He is completely accepting and affirming toward you. You're part of His household. He adores you just like you are.

God is always gracious and gentle toward you. Think about this: There's nothing you can do to make God like you any more than He does right now. There's nothing you can do to cause God to like you any *less* than He does right now. Do you know why? Because you are His.

The first time I went on a date, I was a 16-year-old boy. On the Friday before I was to have my first date, I took my dad's car to the backyard, and I washed it and cleaned it inside and out. I wanted to have a clean car so she'd like me. I took a shower—put on my clean clothes. I even put on a tie. All because I wanted her to like me. I put hair cream on my hair and slicked it back. I wanted to look good. I put on some cologne so I would smell good, because I wanted her to like me. I got to her house 30 minutes early, I knocked on her door, and her mother told me she wasn't ready yet. But I didn't mind waiting. I wanted her to like me. When she came down, I opened the car door for her. I was doing everything to make her like me. I dated that girl for three years and then I married her in 1973 and I've been married to her ever since.

After I was married, I said to myself, *I don't have to do all that stuff anymore. She's mine now. I don't have to make her like me by what I do.* So I stopped treating her that way. Things changed. After about a year of marriage, our marriage was in big trouble. I knew that the only one who could salvage our marriage was God. So I began to pray. I'd pray the same thing every night: "Oh, God! You've got to change that woman!" One night the Lord spoke to me and said, "No, Steve. I need to change *you*." And He did change me, and I began to love my wife as I needed to love her. I've been married to her all this time, but I treat her like I did when we first fell in love. The difference is, I don't do it so she'll like me. I do it because I love her.

That's how it is with God. He has seen you at your worst. Nothing you do or don't do for Him will change the way He feels about you. But as you realize how much He loves you, you'll *want* to serve Him. He's loving, affirming, gracious, and gentle. He not only loves you, He likes you. Nothing is going to change that fact.

In your mind, what is the difference between somebody loving you and *liking* you?

_____

_____

What does it mean to you to know that God not only loves you, but also likes you? How does that change the way you think about Him?

_____

_____

One day I was looking through the book of Psalms and noted all the verses I had underlined as I had read them. I decided to type and string them all together, as if one verse followed the other. So I typed the verses and read them, and it was powerful. It was like reading a love letter from my heavenly Father! Read that letter *slowly* in the paragraphs that follow. Allow Him to speak to your heart today. Listen to His voice and feel His love as you read.

A Love Note from Your Father, Taken from the Psalms

My dear child,

I am with you. (46:7) Stop striving and know that I am God. (46:10) I have chosen your inheritance for you. (47:4) I rule over everything. (47:8) Remember Israel—they didn't possess the land by their own swords. It wasn't their hand that saved them. It was my right hand and my arm and the light of my presence. I favored them. (44:3) So it is with you—I have poured out grace on your lips and will bless you forever. (45:2)

Psalm 46:7
Psalm 46:10; 47:4
Psalm 47:8

Psalm 44:3

Psalm 45:2

I will always guide you, until the day you die. (48:14) You thought I was just like you. (50:21) But my lovingkindness endures all day long, every day. (52:1) Know this—I am for you. (56:9) My lovingkindness toward you is higher than the heavens. (57:10) Stay with me and take refuge under the shelter of my wings. (61:4)

Psalm 48:14
Psalm 50:21
Psalm 52:1
Psalm 56:9
Psalm 57:10
Psalm 61:4

Trust in me at all times and pour out your heart before me. (62:8) I am the one who bears your burdens. I am your salvation and am the God of deliverance for you. (68:19-20) I will show Myself strong in the way I act on your behalf. (68:28) Just trust me and praise me more and more. (71:14)

Psalm 62:8
Psalm 68:19-20
Psalm 68:28
Psalm 71:14

Listen to what I am saying—I speak peace to you, my godly one. (85:8) Your springs of joy are to be found in me. (87:7) I will satisfy you every morning with my lovingkindness. (90:14) When you find anxious thoughts multiplying in your mind, my consolation will delight your soul. So be glad. (94:19)

Psalm 85:8
Psalm 87:7
Psalm 90:14
Psalm 94:19

Psalm 102:27
Psalm 103:19
Psalm 104:34
Psalm 107:20
Psalm 115:3
Psalm 116:5-6
Psalm 119:89

I never change. (102:27) My sovereignty rules over all. (103:19) Meditate on that and I'll be pleased. (104:34) I have sent my word and healed you and delivered you from your destructions. (107:20) I am God. I do whatever I please (115:3) and it pleases me to be gracious and compassionate and to preserve you. (116:5-6) What I have said is settled in heaven. (119:89)

Psalm 130:3-4

I don't count sins, or else nobody could stand. (130:3-4) You are forgiven and my lovingkindness is everlasting. My lovingkindness is everlasting. My lovingkindness is everlasting!

Psalm 136
Psalm 138:8

(Psalm 136 says this 26 times.) I will accomplish the things that concern you. (138:8) I know you—when you sit down and get up, what you think. I carefully watch over you as you move through your day and then sleep at night. I am intimately

Psalm 139:1-4

acquainted with everything about you. (139:1-4) I wrote the script for every day of your life before you lived a single one

Psalm 139:16
Psalm 142:3

of them. (139:16) I know your path and the way where you will walk. (142:3)

Psalm 149:4

And my child...I do take such pleasure in you! (149:4)

With eternal love,
Your proud Father

Read this letter from Psalms a second time and underline the words that particularly speak to you today. This isn't an imaginary letter. Your Father really wrote it. Will you believe Him and accept His love for you? Tell Him so.

At the beginning of the week, I mentioned there were two areas we need to address in order to fully experience the grace walk. Maybe you have learned this week that God is nothing like you have imagined Him to be. You have seen that He is in a good mood toward you. You've come to know He isn't sitting up in heaven, distant from you, critiquing your every move and waiting for you to blow it. God is thrilled with you as His child.

Day Four

Today and tomorrow I want you to consider a second aspect of who God is. This issue has to do with His forgiving nature. Many Christians have failed to fully understand the scope of God's forgiveness toward them. If you aren't completely aware of the extent of His forgiveness toward you, it will be hard to fully experience the grace walk. You will be spiritually crippled to the extent that you don't believe you are fully forgiven.

It is important to understand exactly what happened at salvation. When we became Christians, we received two things that make all the difference in our lives.

God's Mercy

At salvation, we received mercy. Thankfully, we didn't get His justice when we trusted Him. Justice is when you get what you deserve. Considering the sin nature we had when we were born, what do any of us deserve? All of us deserved to be separated from Him for eternity. That would be just. But we didn't get justice—we received mercy. Mercy is when we don't get what we deserve.

2 Corinthians 4:1

Ephesians 2:4

Second Corinthians 4:1 says, "Since we have this ministry, as we received mercy, we do not lose heart." Ephesians 2:4 speaks of "God, who is rich in mercy." It is because of His mercy that He forgave your sins. It doesn't matter what your sin is, by the blood of Jesus there is mercy.

God's Grace

There is a big difference between mercy and grace, as the following illustration demonstrates. Imagine that I am exceeding the speed limit and I'm pulled over by a policeman. There is no question of my guilt. But suppose that the officer decides that, even though I am guilty, he won't give me the ticket I deserve. That would be mercy. He did not give me what I rightfully deserved.

> *Jesus didn't come to just forgive your sins, He came to give you life.*

Mercy is when we don't receive what we deserve. Grace, on the other hand, is when we receive something we don't deserve. For instance, what if, before he got back in his car, the policeman had turned back and handed me a hundred-dollar bill and said, "Here. Take this with you." *That* would have been grace! He would have been giving me something I didn't deserve.

Do you see the spiritual application? God's mercy has caused Him to forgive us of our sins, but His grace has caused Him to give us the life of Jesus. Jesus didn't come to just forgive your sins, He came to give you life.

Look at the following verses and underline the phrases that tell you Jesus wants to do more than forgive sins.

> *God so loved the world, that He gave His only begotten Son, that whoever believes in Him shall not perish, but have eternal life (John 3:16).*

John 3:16

> *He who believes in the Son has eternal life (John 3:36).*

John 3:36

John 10:10

I came that they may have life, and have it abundantly (John 10:10).

These verses don't say anything about God giving us forgiveness. What do they teach that Jesus came to give us?

_____

_____

Jesus came to give us life! By His mercy, He has forgiven us. However, forgiveness is the secondary matter in salvation. He forgave us *so that* He could give us Divine life!

He has shown us mercy by forgiving all our sins. Many Christians don't know that they were totally forgiven. Look at Colossians 2:13-14:

Colossians 2:13-14

> *When you were dead in your transgressions and the uncircumcision of your flesh, He made you alive together with Him, having forgiven us all our transgressions, having canceled out the certificate of debt consisting of decrees against us, which was hostile to us; and He has taken it out of the way, having nailed it to the cross.*

Having forgiven us *all our transgressions*. The certificate of debt to which Paul refers is an invoice, a bill we owe. The Bible says that Jesus took the debt we owed for our sin and He bore that debt on the cross.

Think about the sins you believe have been the worst ones of your lifetime. Can you identify them? The Bible says that those sins were once written on a "certificate of debt," a phrase that today could be translated as an "invoice showing what you owe." Look at the invoice below:

Invoice for Sins

~

Payable in Eternity

1.

2.

3.

4. *An itemized list of all your sins on record in Heaven's Bookkeeping Department*

TOTAL:

Think of the three sins you believe are the worst ones you have committed in your lifetime. In the space above, write the initials of these three sins. Look at them. Read the fourth entry on the invoice. Left to ourselves, we must one day account for every sin we have ever committed in this lifetime.

Look again at Colossians 2:13-14. What does the Bible say about the invoice (certificate of debt) represented above?

Colossians 2:13-14

_____

_____

Colossians 2:13-14

The instrument by which God did away with the debt you owed for your sins was the cross of Jesus Christ. By His death on the cross, your debt for sin has been paid in full. With a bold pen, draw a cross over the entire certificate of debt represented here. Then write the words *Paid in Full by Jesus Christ* across the invoice.

End your study today by affirming to your Father in prayer that, because you are a Christian, He has forgiven you for all your sins. If you struggle with this idea, read Colossians 2:13-14 while personalizing it by using first-person pronouns. Pray it to God as a prayer. Say it out loud to yourself as a promise from Him. He has forgiven you all your transgressions!

Imagine that before you were born, God saw your life from start to finish. He saw everything you would ever do, every sin you would ever commit. He made a list of every one of those sins. All of them— every sinful thought, word, or deed was recorded. Then He took that bill, that invoice, and He placed it on Jesus at the cross. There they were paid for, in full. You learned in yesterday's study that this scenario isn't imaginary. It literally happened!

How many of your sins did God know about before you were born? All of them. How many of your sins did He place on Jesus Christ? All of them. How many of your sins was Jesus punished for? All of them. And when Jesus said, "It is finished. It is paid in full," how many of your sins was He counting? All of them. Later on, when you trusted Christ and God forgave you, how many of your sins were forgiven? All of them. Your sins have all been for- given—even the ones you haven't committed yet.

You might wonder how your future sins could have been forgiven when you haven't even committed them. Let me ask you another question, "How could Jesus have paid for your sins when you hadn't even been born?" After all, they were *all* future sins when He paid for them on the cross, weren't they?

The answer to that question hinges on our understanding of time. Time doesn't tie the hands of God. He stands above it, unable to be contained by it. He lives in the "eternal now" and sees all of history at once.

Someone has defined time as "duration measured by succession." As humans, we experience life *sequentially,* but God stands outside time and sees all things *simultaneously.* He sees your whole lifetime at once. He knows all your sins and is able to place them into Jesus at the cross all at one time. All of your sins have been forgiven. All of them.

License to Sin?

Some people may respond like this: "Well, if you tell a Christian that all his sins are already forgiven even before he commits them, what would keep him from just living a lifestyle of sin?" Remember, the person who loved to sin has died with Christ. When you were baptized into Jesus, you were baptized into His death. Why don't we go out and sin? *Because that's not what we want to do!* We don't want to live a lifestyle of sin, because God has given us a new nature.

> We are now one with Jesus Christ, and nothing will ever change that.

We are now one with Jesus Christ, and nothing will ever change that. There's nothing we can do to cause ourselves to be closer to God or farther from Him. He has already forgiven all of your sins, and you've been joined together with Him. You can never again be far from God because He is in you. You can't get closer to God than you already are. He is your very life. There's nothing you can do now to cause God to condemn you.

I'm going to make a statement I hope you'll understand—because this will liberate you. *God never becomes angry with you.*

Let's reason this out. What would make God angry? Your answer is likely to be, "Sin—that would make God angry."

That's true. Sin is what causes God to be angry. Now, how many of your sins did God see before you were born? All of them. How many of your sins did God place on Jesus at the cross? All of them. How many of your sins came under the full wrath of God at the cross? All of them.

Your sins were judged at the cross. All of God's anger was poured out at the cross. When you were forgiven of your sin, you were forgiven fully and completely. God is not like a human being. He's not going to get angry again about something He has already forgiven. When it's forgiven, it's forgiven. The reason you think that God gets angry is because that is how a human would be. But don't project your humanity on God. His ways are not our ways.

You can't even *disappoint* God. Disappointment is the result of an unfulfilled expectation. You expect one thing, but you get something else. You cannot disappoint God because God doesn't expect anything. He already *knows* everything. He will never say to you, "I expected something different from you." He knew. You didn't know, but He knew.

When I say you can't disappoint God, don't think I'm saying it doesn't grieve the heart of your Father when you sin. Of course it does. He hates to see you do things He knows will hurt you. But it didn't surprise Him that you did it.

You might exclaim over something you did, "I can't believe I did that!" But God will say, "I knew it all along." He knew the day He saved you that you would do that thing. He knew everything you would do before you were even born.

Do you know what it will do for you if you realize that your sins are forgiven, past, present, and future? It will give you the freedom to take your eyes off sin and put them completely on Jesus Christ.

> *Don't project your humanity on God. His ways are not our ways.*

A Christian feels condemned when he feels alienated from God and believes that God is impatiently frowning at him. But condemnation doesn't come from God. He simply won't do that to you.

Although God doesn't condemn you, He will convict you. Conviction draws your heart back toward Him. Condemnation will cause you to feel alienated from Him. Conviction brings the understanding that He's not mad, but that His arms are open and He is concerned about you. He wants the best for you.

When you've sinned, you don't have to beg God to forgive you. When we beg and plead for forgiveness, we are really saying that the work of Jesus Christ on the cross was not sufficient. When you sin, you acknowledge it, but not so you can get forgiveness.

Are you on track with a clear understanding of the difference between conviction and condemnation? How would you describe the difference between the two?

_____

_____

We need to understand the complete pardon that we have. You are fully forgiven. Stop being so sin-conscious. Does this mean we are careless about sin? Of course not, but it does mean that we aren't to obsess over the subject of sin. We are to be obsessed with Jesus Christ. When you do commit a sin, the Holy Spirit will convict you. When He does so, acknowledge it and go on.

If Christians really believed that, it would empower us with such joy that we would reach the world for Christ. When Jesus said, "It is finished," did He mean it? Was it true? Do you believe it? Live in the freedom of complete forgiveness and of who God really is.

Let this truth take root deep within you. Embrace each statement. Indicate that you accept its truth by initialing beside each thought.

☐ *God not only loves me, He likes me.*

☐ *God is so delighted with me that He is dancing around and singing because He can't hold back the joy.*

☐ *God is smiling at me.*

☐ *God never gets mad at me.*

☐ *I never disappoint God.*

☐ *The sins of my entire lifetime are forgiven.*

8

LIVING THE CHRISTIAN
LIFE CAN BE EASY

Matthew 11:30

Jesus said that when we come to Him we will discover that His yoke is easy and His burden is light (see Matthew 11:30). Living the Christian life is impossible to do in our own strength, but as we allow Christ to live through us we discover why He said His yoke is easy. He will live the life we could never live on our own.

During this final week of study, we are going to conclude with an examination of a few important practical aspects of continuing your walk in grace. How do you move on from this point? To answer that question, I want to address some final practical matters related to your experiencing the grace walk in the days ahead.

This week we are going to spend a couple of days considering how to handle negative feelings that contradict the truth of God's Word. Then we are going to examine the "grace way" of knowing God's will. On day four, we will look at prayer and Bible study through the grace lens. Then on the last day, we'll see what evangelism and the church look like when we are experiencing the grace walk.

When Feelings and Faith Collide

When I first began to learn about my identity in Christ, it was hard for me to accept some of these truths. Even when I saw the truth in the Bible, my feelings refused to align themselves with what God's Word says. Do you find that to be the case in your life too?

What are the truths taught in this book that you have struggled to accept? List them:

_____

_____

_____

_____

Unless you have seen the truths you just wrote proven in this book by the Bible, don't change your mind. However, if you *do* see the things you listed taught in Scripture, then you have a decision to make.

As we have progressed though this study, I have repeatedly asked you, "Do you believe the Bible?" The reason for my asking that question is because I realize that much of what I have said may contradict what you have felt to be true. Maybe some of what has been discussed even contradicts what you have been taught along the way.

For that reason, I have used an abundance of Scripture. Scripture is the final authority in the life of a believer. Even so, sometimes when we see something in the Bible we haven't seen before, our old beliefs are so firmly entrenched that we still struggle to believe it.

I challenge you, if you've struggled with some of the things I've shared with you, get into the Bible for yourself. Don't take my word for it. Study the Bible. Read other books on the subject. Continue to dig deeply and don't stop until you are persuaded one way or the other. The truth can always stand up to scrutiny. See for yourself.

> *Scripture is the final authority in the life of a believer.*

While it's wrong to be gullible, and you don't want to instantly and indiscriminately take a person's word for something without checking it out in the Scriptures, there is another error that people can fall into as well. They can refuse to be teachable.

Just because a teaching doesn't fit their tradition, or doesn't line up comfortably with what they've always thought, they instantly reject it without giving it any serious consideration or without examining the Word of God for themselves. I want to challenge you to be teachable. Just because something is new *to us* doesn't mean it is new.

Surely we realize we don't know everything there is to know. Surely none of us would profess to have perfect knowledge. All of us have room to grow and learn.

> *Truth is whatever God says, regardless of what I might feel and think.*

Dealing with Negative Feelings

Because our feelings sometimes contradict the truth, we need to know how to deal with those feelings. A first step in that process has to do with understanding the meaning of truth.

Consider this definition: *Truth is whatever God says, regardless of what I might feel and think.* Is that definition acceptable to you? The ultimate authority is the Word of God. Our own feelings or thoughts are secondary to whatever God says.

Let's apply this definition of truth to the journey you have taken during these eight weeks toward experiencing the grace walk. I'll use one point we have studied to illustrate how we are to deal with our feelings.

Consider the truth you have learned about the fact that we are righteous. Right now every believer is holy. That is an objective fact. However, many of us don't *feel* holy. The biblical teaching that every Christian is holy even contradicts what some people have been taught in church. They have learned that we *achieve* holiness by our actions. Nothing could be further from the truth. So what are we to do if our feelings contradict truth?

1. Decide what source will be your final authority. When you recognize that the Bible teaches you are holy, but you don't feel that way, you must choose what to accept as your authority—the Bible or your feelings. Some people are driven by their feelings, but that is a dangerous way to live. Don't allow your feelings to form your theology! Trust God's Word for that.

Consider the following two questions and note the link between them.

How would you answer a new believer who said, "I just don't feel like a Christian"?

_____

_____

Apply your answer to yourself if you are thinking, *I just don't feel holy.* What would you tell yourself?

_____

_____

The common element in both questions is feelings. The foundational issue isn't how we feel, is it? The key point centers on what we are going to depend on as our ultimate source of authority. We must choose to override our feelings and embrace what the Bible says.

As a young man, Billy Graham struggled with the idea of whether or not he could really trust the Bible as his own final authority. Knowing this matter had to be settled in his mind if he ever hoped to preach with authority and power, he wrestled with his doubts until one day, alone in the woods, he prayed, "Oh God, I cannot prove certain things. I cannot answer some of the questions my friends are asking. Yet, here and now I am ready to accept the Bible by faith as the Word of God." And the rest, as they say, is history.

Will you write your own prayer to that effect in the space below?

In tomorrow's study, we will consider another step toward dealing with negative feelings. But for now, conclude today's study with the prayer of affirmation you have written above. Thank God that His Word is trustworthy.

Yesterday I challenged you to deal with thoughts and feelings that contradict what you've learned during this study by affirming that the Bible will be your final authority. Today we will consider the next steps in dealing with feelings that conflict with biblical truth.

2. Determine what the truth is. This is the second key to dealing with negative feelings. Back to the example I've given about holiness. The Bible says you are holy. Think about the times you have sinned. You don't feel very holy then, do you?

Day Two

When you've committed a sin, you may feel like a *vile* person, not a *holy* person. You feel unrighteous. What do you do about this feeling? You determine the truth about the matter based on what the Bible says.

You don't determine the truth by your feelings, but by the source of authority you have put your trust in, which is the Word of God. So at a time when everything in my circumstances and emotions tells me I am unholy, I have to ask myself what the Bible says. What does the Bible say about this matter of the Christian's holiness? As practice, write a few verses in the space below that indicate Christians are holy. Look back through this study so far. You have looked in detail at several places where the Scripture says, in no uncertain terms, that you are holy. (See the chapters for weeks three and four.) List a few of the verses here:

_____

_____

_____

So when you have a negative feeling that contradicts the truth, you immediately ask yourself, *What does the Bible say?* That way you are able to identify the truth in clear, concrete terms. (Can you see that this is one reason why Bible study is important for the Christian?)

In this grace walk, you have determined that the Bible will be your final source of authority. You have determined what is the truth from the Bible. The next step is an important one in overcoming negative emotions.

> *When confronted in my thoughts with the lie, I simply say, "No! I am not unholy. I am not vile."*

3. Renounce the lie. You recognize that your feelings are influencing you to believe a lie. I may sin and, because of that, I no longer feel holy. That may lead to the *thought* that tells me that I am not holy. An inner voice tells me so in such a convincing tone that I must *choose* to renounce the lie.

2 Corinthians 10:5

Second Corinthians 10:5 teaches us that very thing. It says,

> *We are destroying speculations and every lofty thing raised up against the knowledge of God, and we are taking every thought captive to the obedience of Christ.*

That is an important key in continuing in grace. Renounce the lie!

When confronted in my thoughts with the lie, I simply say, "No! I am not unholy. I am not vile." Our feelings may create a subjective sense within us that we aren't holy, but the objective truth of God's Word is that we *are* holy, despite our feelings to the contrary.

4. Affirm the truth. After identifying the truth and renouncing the lie, I then consciously affirm the truth: "I *am* holy. I *am* righteous. The truth isn't determined by what I feel right now. My confidence isn't in my feelings or negative thoughts. I trust God's Word. Jesus, You are my holiness!"

I may not feel it, but because the Bible says so, it is true! Jesus said in John 8:32, "You will know the truth, and the truth will set you free." For that reason, we need to lay hold of the truth and refuse to let go when negative feelings and doubting thoughts seem to relentlessly assault us!

John 8:32

Pause here for a moment to practice what you are learning. The following exercise will help you.

What negative feeling or doubtful thought has attacked you at times?

_____

_____

_____

What is the truth about the matter? (In other words, what does the Bible say about it?)

_____

_____

_____

_____

What is the lie you are being tempted to embrace? Renounce it in writing.

_____

_____

_____

Affirm in writing the truth about the matter. Make this affirmation personal.

_____

_____

_____

5. Walk in the truth regardless of what you feel. Once you have taken the steps of faith already discussed, your feelings may or may not instantly change. Most of the time they don't, but that is okay. You don't live by feelings. You live by faith.

What do you do now? You walk in the truth regardless of your feelings. You just move forward, trusting Christ as you go. For instance, you may pray, "Father, you say I am holy. I'm standing on what You say." Then, you get up and begin to act like a holy person. To do otherwise would be hypocritical. After all, you *are* a holy person! So act like who you are. What you feel is irrelevant.

You will discover that as you depend on the sufficiency of the indwelling Christ and affirm God's Word, your mind will gradually

Galatians 2:20

be renewed. Eventually your feelings may change. Sometimes they never do, but that doesn't really matter because you are appropriating the truth of the Word of God for your situation.

Make sure you understand this: *Feelings are incidental, not fundamental.* Your feelings may be the same as when you started, but that doesn't matter. They may gradually change or they may not. Either way, keep walking in the truth.

Assuming that the Bible is your final authority, what are the four things you are to do with negative feelings?

1.

2.

3.

4.

I don't want you to see these items as a formula. Don't try to turn it into some kind of legalistic magic. I want you to see this as a perspective, just the natural way you live out of the life of Jesus Christ. The more you believe the truth, the more your actions will change in response to it.

To continue on in experiencing the grace walk, it is important to know what God wants us to do with our lives. Questions about knowing God's will are among the most common I receive as I travel in ministry. We all want to know that we are in the center of His will for our lives. But how can we know for sure?

There seems to be so much confusion about knowing the will of God. I hope that by this point in your study you have come to realize that the nature of grace means God has taken the burden off you to figure it all out. Grace is one-sided. Everything is up to Him. All we need to do is receive by responding to Him in faith and obedience.

There are three key points in knowing God's will that I want you to consider today. Work your way slowly through each of these and allow them to renew your mind.

1. God's will is fulfilled through you by Jesus Christ

Is Jesus Christ living in and through you? When He expresses His life through you, there is no way you can get out of God's will. The will of God for you is Christ! When you understand that God's will is Jesus Christ in you, you will find that His will is not something to find, but to be fulfilled.

Romans 12:1-2

As you trust Jesus Christ moment by moment you will prove the will of God. How could you possibly get out of God's will if the life of Jesus is the source of your behavior? What is your responsibility in this matter? Romans 12:1-2 gives the answer:

I urge you, brethren, by the mercies of God, to present your bodies a living and holy sacrifice, acceptable to God, which is your spiritual service of worship. And do not be conformed to this world, but be transformed by the renewing of your mind, so that you may prove what the will of God is, that which is good and acceptable and perfect.

The Bible says there is a way to "prove what the will of God is." According to this passage, what is your responsibility in proving the will of God in your life?

_____

_____

There is no need for you to feel anxious about God's will for your life. He will make it clear to you as you continually trust Jesus to be who He is in you and through you. Navigating your way through life isn't your responsibility. The Spirit of Jesus Christ within you will guide you. Just relax and trust Him.

Are you feeling anxious right now about a decision of any kind? Is there anything about which you want to know God's will? Maybe you are feeling anxious about someone else needing to know God's will. Define your anxiety and how you are feeling about it.

_____

_____

Do you remember what to do with negative thoughts and feelings? Identify and renounce any lies you are believing about finding God's will. Then replace the lies with the truth.

The lie is:

_____

_____

The truth is:

_____

_____

2. You have the mind of Christ

The second aspect of knowing God's will is to understand that you have the mind of Christ. Since Jesus lives through you, He will guide your thoughts as you trust Him. It isn't necessary to worry about choices. Simply trust in Jesus and, in faith, make a choice.

A friend of mine who leads a ministry once had a choice to make. The deadline for his decision was quickly approaching. He asked the Lord what He wanted him to do, but as the deadline for the decision neared, he didn't have a clear leading from the Lord. He was beginning to feel some anxiety and finally cried out, "Lord, what do You want me to do?" He finally heard the Lord say, "I want you to decide." We have the mind of Christ. We can decide, knowing it is Jesus in us who is expressing His thoughts and desires through us as we trust in Him.

Imagine yourself standing in the center of a large field, consisting of hundreds of acres. You can see the horizon in every direction. To the west you see the ocean. To the east you see a beautiful mountain range. On the north is a lushly wooded forest. Looking south, you see a beautiful lake shaded by overhanging trees. As you turn in a complete circle, there are many small points on the horizon that catch your eye. You can go to any of those spots. Many look interesting. Some don't.

Those points on the horizon represent your choices in life. Which should you choose? If you are trusting Christ within you, the answer is easy. Choose the place you desire. It is important that you are enjoying your intimate union with Jesus while you choose. In other words, don't act independently of Him. Trust Him to guide your thoughts. If that is the case, *then decide*. Make a decision!

Have you selected the point on the horizon to which you want to go? Okay, then run! Run there as fast as you can. Run with excitement and joyful anticipation. When you reach the spot you have selected, do you know what you will find? Jesus is standing there.

> *Don't act independently of Him. Trust Him to guide your thoughts… Make a decision!*

As you draw near, you see His arms outstretched toward you. He is laughing with joy. You draw near enough to hear His voice. "Come on!" He says. "Run! Run! I've been waiting for you to get here! This is *exactly* where I wanted you to be!" "Lord!" you exclaim, "I'm so glad You're here! No matter what this place holds for me, I *know* the Father's purpose will be done because You drew me here and will be with me at every moment."

This Christian life is so much more enjoyable than we have often experienced it to be. You don't have to agonize your way through the decision-making process. Just relax and trust the Christ who indwells you to lead you.

> *Relax! This life isn't a test, it's a rest.*

Relax! This life isn't a test, it's a rest. "The test has already been given and Jesus has passed it with flying colors." You can act in faith about God's will, not in fear. Make choices in faith, knowing that God is guiding your thoughts.

Describe the difference in the way a legalist might approach knowing God's will and the way a person walking in grace will approach knowing His will.

_____

_____

_____

How will understanding that you have the mind of Christ change the way you make decisions in the future?

_____

_____

_____

Some may ask, "Isn't prayer a part of this process?" Prayer is as natural to the Christian as breathing. Do we pray as we make our decisions? Of course! Prayer, open doors of opportunity, our own desires—all these fit together in knowing the mind of Christ for our lives. The key here is to understand that these aren't pieces of a puzzle *we* must put together to know God's will. They are the components of a beautiful picture that God is actively painting to show us His beautiful plan for us. We can simply relax and watch the Artist as He reveals His plan for our lives.

3. Don't second-guess God's will after you have acted in faith

A big mistake Christians make concerning the will of God is to assume that somehow they have missed it if things don't turn out the way they had expected. Does it mean you have missed God's will if that happens? Absolutely not!

Do you remember the imaginary field I mentioned earlier? Imagine for a moment that I made the choice to go to the beach. I opted against the mountains, the lake, and the forest. It was the beach that drew me toward it.

So I find myself there, believing God has led me into His perfect will. Picture me resting in my hammock on my beach, when I begin to notice a dark cloud out on the horizon. Little by little the dark cloud gets bigger and comes nearer—it sure looks like a storm headed my way.

Finally the storm hits, but it's not just a storm. It's a hurricane. When I first got there, the sun was shining and everything was beautiful. But now the wind is blowing and I'm holding on to that palm tree trying to keep from getting blown away. Everything around me is being devastated, and I'm holding on for dear life.

The temptation at this point may be to say, "Oh, no! I must have missed the will of God. I thought the Lord brought me here, but look at what's going on." Now I'm tempted to second-guess God's will because it didn't turn out the way I thought it would.

Does it mean we have missed God's will when circumstances don't develop the way we anticipated? Absolutely not. It only means that God had a different agenda for our situation than we thought. He simply chose not to tell us in advance what the outcome would be, but to allow us to discover it as we moved forward.

When you have made a choice and acted in faith, and have passed through the door of decision, do not look back and second-guess yourself. You can trust that the Holy Spirit will guide you as He has promised. Results from your decisions that aren't what you thought they would be in no way indicate a wrong decision.

Some might wonder, "But what if I acted out of my flesh when I made my choice?" Let me tell you another wonderful thing about God—He's bigger than your wrong choices. Daniel 4:35 says,

Daniel 4:35

> *All the inhabitants of the earth are accounted as nothing, But He does according to His will in the host of heaven and among the inhabitants of earth; and no one can ward off His hand or say to Him, "What have You done?"*

Don't punish yourself for your choices. Your sovereign Father has redeemed your choices. When you get to heaven and see the tapestry of your life, you will see that even the dark threads contribute to the beauty of the piece of art that is your life.

Do you want to be in the center of God's will? Then abide in Jesus Christ and let Him live through you. Trust Him continuously and boldly make choices. He won't let you veer off the path He has planned for you.

As you end your study today, think about decisions you have to make. Ask your Father to give you confidence to trust Him and move forward in faith.

Think about choices you have made in the past that afterward appeared to be wrong ones. Apply Daniel 4:35 to your situation. Write here how the verse applies to that choice.

Daniel 4:35

_____

_____

_____

_____

_____

_____

_____

_____

_____

_____

_____

We are moving closer to the end of our journey toward the grace walk experience. The goal this week is to equip you for the road ahead in your life. You've learned how to deal with negative emotions and doubtful thoughts. Yesterday, you discovered how to move forward in faith, trusting the indwelling Christ to keep you in the perfect will of God.

Today I want you to be equipped to experience Bible study and prayer from a grace-filled perspective. First, consider the way you relate to the Bible. A legalistic approach to Scripture will rob you of the blessing of experiencing Him through His Word.

Think about the answer to this question before you read further. Answer honestly. Why do you read your Bible?

_____

_____

Living by the Bible

Some Christians view the Bible as little more than a guidebook, an operator's manual. "The Bible," they say, "will teach you how to live." While that assessment of Scripture isn't altogether wrong, it is far from complete.

The Bible is not an operator's manual. Grace will cause you to see it more like a picture album. When we approach the Bible through grace, we come to it to see and experience Jesus. Reading the Bible becomes like the experience of looking through the family album. You find yourself saying, "Look! It's Jesus! Isn't He beautiful!"

Does the Bible equip you for living? Yes. As you come to know Jesus He will equip you for living through what you learn in Scripture. But that is not its main function.

A legalist reduces the Bible to a set of moral values. He reads the Bible and then tries to live by those values. But a grace-oriented approach to the Scripture will cause you to come to it looking for Jesus. Once you've seen Him there, you *will* be changed. Nobody encounters Jesus and remains the same.

Maybe you have had trouble consistently reading your Bible until now because you saw it as an operator's manual. If so, reject that perspective now and ask the Holy Spirit to renew your mind to the truth so you begin to see it as an album filled with portraits and love letters from Jesus.

Learning the Bible

I grew up believing that we needed to study the Bible so we could better know its contents. Again, this isn't completely untrue, but there is a deeper issue at hand that we need not to miss. The fundamental question revolves around *why* we want to know the contents of the Bible.

The Pharisees knew the Bible better than many Christians will ever know it. However, it isn't enough to learn what it says. If we come to the Bible just to gain Bible content, that can actually be dangerous. The apostle Paul said that knowledge alone makes you proud and arrogant. Under legalism, a person comes to the Bible only to learn what it says. He takes great pride in knowing Bible content.

Under grace we come to the Bible to meet Jesus. Do we learn the Bible? Yes. Does it change us? Yes. But our goal as we approach the Bible is to gaze on Jesus.

John 5:30-40

Read John 5:30-40 in your own Bible. The Pharisees read and memorized the Scriptures for the wrong reason. What was their reason for reading Scripture?

_____

_____

Jesus said in this passage that the Scripture serves as a signpost directing the readers. Where does it point those who read it?

_____

_____

How to Read Your Bible

Do you want to read your Bible and see Jesus in it? The following guidelines, taken from my book *The Godward Gaze* (Harvest House Publishers, 2003) may be helpful in developing a grace-filled approach to the Scripture. Don't view these guidelines as a legalistic formula for Bible-reading. They are simply ways that many people have found helpful to satisfy their hunger to encounter Jesus Christ through Scripture.

1. Before you read, pray and ask the Lord to reveal Himself to you through His Word. Before you even pick up your Bible, pause and pray. This isn't a test to determine your spirituality. It isn't an assignment you will either pass or fail. There is nothing you can do to generate an encounter with Jesus. We all know from experience that it is possible to read the Bible and find no more benefit from it at the moment than if we were reading the whole New York Stock Exchange report in the daily newspaper. Ask Jesus to reveal Himself to you as you read.

2. Ask the Holy Spirit to guide you concerning where you are to read. As you are learning to read your Bible from a perspective of grace, He probably won't direct you to obscure passages that are hard to understand. When I was a child, I would sometimes flip my Bible open to a random passage and begin to read wherever my eyes fell. Now I trust the Holy Spirit to lead me as I read God's Word.

The Christ who indwells you will guide you to meet Him in His Word. Some have asked about the specifics of my own Bible reading. I read from the Psalms every day. I am often led to Paul's epistles. I regularly read from the Gospels too. That is the path I am on. Yours may look like mine or it may be different. Ask for divine guidance as you approach God's Word, and you will receive it.

> *The Christ who indwells you will guide you to meet Him in His Word.*

3. Read slowly and with a prayerful heart. When you read this way, you will sometimes find that a verse seems to jump right off the page and you *know* that, through it, God is talking to you. Don't worry about how much you read. Your goal isn't so much to read the Bible as it is to allow the Bible to read you!

Read your Bible slowly, prayerfully, and with an open heart. You will discover that Jesus will speak to you as you patiently read and wait. When He does speak, meditate on what He has spoken by turning it over and over in your mind until you have tasted its last drop of nectar.

4. Combine your faith and your imagination as you read.
Project yourself mentally into the passage you read. Do you know how you get caught up in a movie when you watch it? You feel the sadness of the lover with the broken heart. You share a sense of fear the heroine in danger feels. You sense the thrill of the hero when he wins out over the bad guy. In a sense, you become a part of the movie while you watch it.

Read your Bible that way. In reality, you can much more readily identify with the Bible characters than you can imaginary characters in a screenplay. After all, the Bible characters were real people, just like you. The same way God worked in their lives, He wants to work in your life. It isn't "pretending" when you project yourself into these biblical stories because, in some way, their story *is* your story.

> *Bible characters were real people, just like you. The same way God worked in their lives, He wants to work in your life.*

5. Take the word Jesus speaks to you with you throughout your day. Once He has spoken to you and you have meditated on His Word, take that word with you throughout your day. In the midst of your busy schedule, think about what He said to you. Turn it over in your mind again all throughout the day. You may find yourself literally smiling as you think about His intimate words to you through the Bible. As you do, you can be assured of something—He's smiling too.

Now, practice what you have just learned by selecting a passage of Scripture and applying these five guidelines to that passage. After you have done it, record in the space below how it impacted you. If it didn't have a major impact on you, don't worry. Be consistent to read your Bible *for the purpose of meeting Jesus there* and you will learn to see and hear Him in due time.

_____

_____

_____

_____

Praying in Grace

How does grace change our prayer life? When we experience the grace walk, prayer becomes more than an action. It becomes an attitude of continual relationship with God. Before I experienced the grace walk, my prayer life could be characterized as something I did, an action that occurred when I spoke to God. Now prayer is different. It is an attitude of open communion with the Father every moment as I abide in Christ.

Our children say that Melanie and I sometimes talk without speaking. They're right. They have suggested we often read each other's mind. That's not altogether wrong either. We have been married since 1973, and we do know each other's mind fairly often.

Sometimes words aren't even necessary. A glance may be sufficient. As we live together in intimacy, our communication is not labored or even scheduled. It flows naturally out of relationship.

Write a short description of your prayer life as it exists now:

_____

_____

In what ways would you like to see your prayer life be transformed?

_____

_____

Do you want to experience the grace walk in prayer? Stop viewing your prayer life as a set time when you must say certain words to God. There is nothing wrong with a set time to pray if that's what you want to do. But having a "quiet time" for the sake of fulfilling what you may perceive to be your duty to God is empty and wasted time.

Prayer in the Christian life is the conduit by which we experience intimacy with our Savior and Friend. He is the Divine Lover, who wants you to fully know Him and the great passion He has for you. To pray is to rest in His presence, interacting with Him by intimate means that at times will involve words, and at other times not.

Does your prayer life reverberate with a sense of love between you and Jesus? Do you experience your Father's love as you pray? The following suggestions (taken from *The Godward Gaze*) may help you grow toward a greater grace-based lifestyle of prayer.

1. Pray to be freed from a legalistic paradigm about prayer. Ask to have no other motivation to pray than love and a longing to experience Him. If the focus of the teaching you have received about prayer is on how you *should* pray, you probably have been robbed of the joy of heartfelt prayer. Obligation often kills inspiration. Pray that your mind will be renewed concerning the meaning of prayer. Ask the Holy Spirit to awaken within you a growing *desire* to experience divine love and life as you pray.

2. Sit quietly and focus your attention on Jesus Christ. Resist the impulse to immediately begin using words for prayer. Set your mind on the love your heavenly Father has for you. Reject analytical thoughts about what this time is supposed to accomplish. It isn't up to you to accomplish anything. Just turn your heart toward Him in quiet submission and wait.

3. Listen to the gentle prompting of the Holy Spirit. Determine to have no agenda for your time of prayer other than to set your attention upon Him. God's Spirit may gently guide your thoughts into various areas of your life where He wants to act. He may cause you to express prayer for yourself or others using words. However, there may be times when it isn't necessary to frame your request in words.

Sometimes you may find yourself simply recognizing a need and mentally lifting that need upward and laying it at the feet of Jesus, without a word being expressed mentally or vocally. If you don't know what to say, then say nothing. Simply present your requests to Him by imagining you are laying them out before Him.

End your time today by practicing the principles of prayer discussed here. Remember that growth is a gradual process, so be patient as the Holy Spirit helps you grow in the area of prayer. Don't lose hope in this area. You will come to discover that your prayer life is one of the most powerful ways to experience the grace walk.

Here we are at the last stop on our journey toward experiencing the grace walk! Have you seen changes in your thoughts and attitudes about the Christian life during these eight weeks? Experiencing the grace walk is the greatest thing that has ever occurred in my life. I pray that you are finding the same to be true in your own life.

Day Five

What is the biggest area where you have seen spiritual change in your life during this eight-week study?

_____

_____

Remember that this life is a grace *walk*. That indicates we are always in progress. None of us have arrived at the final destination God has planned for us yet. We are all in progress, but you can rest assured He will finish what He has started in you. Understanding who you are in Christ and how to walk in grace isn't the finish line. It is the starting point. As you move forward in grace, you will continue to see your paradigm being changed as the Holy Spirit renews your mind to the truth of grace.

So far this week you have learned how experiencing the grace walk transforms our lives in practical ways. Yesterday we considered how it affects us in the areas of Bible reading and prayer. Today, I want to conclude with a discussion of how grace transforms our perspective on evangelism and the church.

Evangelizing in Grace

It is absolutely liberating to understand evangelism from a grace perspective. For many years I considered evangelism to be the duty I had—the duty to make sure that as many people as possible became Christians. It was up to me to share the gospel with them and see to it that they prayed "the sinner's prayer," thus ensuring that they went to heaven when they died.

How would you define evangelism?

_____

_____

Since coming to experience the grace walk, I have a different definition for evangelism. Now I define evangelism as *an excitement about Jesus Christ that is contagious*. It's that simple.

I don't see it as a *duty* anymore. Now I see it as a *privilege* to participate in God's redemptive program in this world. He will bring people to Himself, with or without me being involved. But the fact is, He loves me so much that He gives me the opportunity to be a part of bringing people into His kingdom. Evangelism is a gift He gives to Christians by allowing us to participate in what He is doing to reach those who don't yet know Him.

Legalism heaps guilt on those who aren't living up to its demands for evangelism. It insists that we *should* witness. Experiencing the grace walk causes us to recognize that we *are* a witness (see Acts 1:8). Grace inflames the desire to witness with our lives, our lips, or both. It ignites compassion toward the lost and motivates the Christian to naturally evangelize with supernatural power.

> *Evangelism...an excitement about Jesus Christ that is contagious.*
>
> Acts 1:8

Grace Motivates Us to Share
a Person, *Not a* Plan

When I was a legalist, my focus toward the lost was on sharing "the plan of salvation." I began by asking the question, "If you were to die today, do you know where you would spend eternity?" If they didn't give the right answer (with confidence), I would proceed to share a four-point plan from the Bible. At the end of the presentation, the person would be asked to make a decision for Christ.

I don't want to be misunderstood at this point. It *is* important to share the Word with unbelievers as we witness to them about Christ. I know that faith comes by hearing the word of God. In no way do I intend to minimize the role of Scripture in evangelism. Yet it is possible to share a "plan" of salvation without making it clear that we are seeking to introduce the lost person to Christ. The goal of evangelism is not to obtain decisions *for* Christ, but to introduce people *to* Christ.

> *The goal of evangelism is not to obtain decisions for Christ, but to introduce people to Christ.*

Effective evangelism doesn't simply leave a person with the knowledge that he is a Christian. Thorough evangelism leaves him in love with a Person named Jesus. It leaves the new Christian with the understanding that his identity has changed through his relationship to Christ. What assurance does the new believer have that he has really been saved? If he was evangelized through a plan of salvation that *ended* with an opportunity for a decision, his only basis for assurance is by looking back to the moment in his past when he made his decision for Christ. If he was made aware that he was entering into an eternal relationship with the living Christ, his assurance of salvation is that he *knows* Christ *right now*.

Have you ever verbally shared the gospel with another person? One of the easiest ways to do so is to tell them your own story. Write your own testimony of salvation on paper and you'll see it isn't hard to share the gospel. Answer the following questions to get you started.

1. What was your life like before you met Jesus Christ?

_____

_____

_____

2. How did you come to know Christ?

_____

_____

_____

3. How has your life changed since you met Christ?

_____

_____

_____

Your answers to these questions will give you the framework for evangelism! There are many good ways to share the gospel with an unbeliever, but there is no bad way. The word *gospel* means "the good news that makes a person's heart so merry that he wants to jump for joy." I'll say it again: There's no bad way to tell good news like that.

Don't view evangelism as something you must do. When you experience the grace walk, you'll find you want to talk to other people about Jesus. Ask Him to give you opportunities to share the gospel with others and relax. It is up to Him to give you both the opportunity and the ability to do it.

Seeing the Church Through Eyes of Grace

Since beginning an itinerant ministry in 1994, I've been in most denominational churches in America and many in other countries. A common flaw I have seen in all groups is the tendency to think that *we* are on the right track and that anybody who doesn't belong to the same group as us is somehow not completely on target. This kind of attitude stands in contradiction to grace in the body of Christ.

Legalism is characterized by an attitude of exclusivity. It sets up an "us-them mentality" and suggests that we are right in our position and others are wrong. Walking in grace has expanded my perception of the church. No group of Christians has a clear focus on all the truth. One group may have a better understanding of one part of the truth, while another group has a clearer understanding of another aspect of spiritual truth. That's why we need each other.

Embodied within the many denominations of the Christian community is the truth, but to think that *we* somehow have it all figured out and nobody else does is the height of arrogance.

Think about the particular church group to which you belong. What are a few things that you appreciate about that group?

_____

_____

_____

Now, think about another group or denomination that is totally different from yours. What are some commendable things you can say about that group?

_____

_____

_____

1 Corinthians 12:12-13

Did you struggle to answer the second question? If so, you may need the Holy Spirit to expand your perspective on the church of Jesus Christ. The apostle Paul used the metaphor of the human body to show the diversity in God's church. In 1 Corinthians 12:12-13, he wrote,

> *Even as the body is one and yet has many members, and all the members of the body, though they are many, are one body, so also is Christ. For by one Spirit we were all baptized into one body, whether Jews or Greeks, whether slaves or free, and we were all made to drink of one Spirit.*

When we experience the grace walk, we will find a Christlike acceptance of those who are different from us. Christians don't have to be clones of each other! Just because somebody else is different from us doesn't mean they are wrong.

I am not suggesting that doctrine is unimportant. There are indispensable tenets that cause every church to be distinctively Christian. However, a grace perspective on the church doesn't demand we all agree on every detail of faith and practice. I have never been a proponent of ecumenicism that throws doctrine out the church window, but there must be room somewhere within the structure of God's church for unity among the various members of the ecclesiastical family. A grace perspective allows diversity among the family of God.

Paul went on to say in 1 Corinthians 12:18-20:

1 Corinthians 12:18-20

> *God has placed the members, each one of them, in the body, just as He desired. If they were all one member, where would the body be? But now there are many members, but one body.*

From God's perspective, His church is one body. Isn't that what Paul is saying? We have been joined together in union with Christ and with each other. We must recognize the distinctions within the members of the body and allow the Head to give direction to the various parts. Legalism wants to make every part of the body be a mouth or a foot or a hand, but the Word of God clearly teaches that each member of the body is responsible to follow the direction of the head.

As members of God's church, we need each other. Legalism separates Christians, but grace draws us together in a loving relationship. We are one in union with Christ. Outward appearances may distinguish us from each other, but at the core we are the same because our very life is Christ.

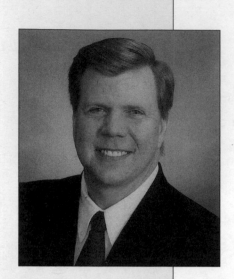

KEEP WALKING!
A Final Word from Steve McVey

Congratulations! You have completed eight weeks of study on the subject of your identity in Christ. You have learned practical truths that will enable you to walk in grace from this day forward. It is my prayer that you see a big difference in your life now. I want to encourage you to do several things as you move forward in your own grace walk.

1. Write me and let me know how your life has been impacted by this study.

It is always encouraging to hear from readers and to discover how their lives have been transformed by God's grace. You may write me at the following address:

Steve McVey
Grace Walk Ministries
PO Box 3669
Riverview, FL 33568

You can also e-mail me through our Web site at www.gracewalk.org. I would be happy to hear from you and to know what God has done in your life as a result of your learning these truths.

2. Continue to study the Bible from a grace perspective so that you can renew your mind.

Living from a paradigm of grace not only requires learning how to walk, but for many of us it requires unlearning some things we have believed in the past. Grace Walk Ministries offers many resources that can help you continue to grow in your own grace walk. Contact us for a complete list of books and audio/video materials to help facilitate your ongoing spiritual growth.

3. Keep your eyes on Christ and don't fall into the snare of legalism.

The current of legalism runs strong in the river of religion. Don't allow yourself to be swept up by its pull. Paul wrote in Galatians 5:1, "It was for freedom that Christ set us free; therefore keep standing firm and do not be subject again to a yoke of slavery." By the cross of Jesus Christ, you have been set free from both sin and empty religion. Stand firm in His grace.

May God continue to bless and guide you as you explore the riches of His grace in Christ Jesus and may you daily be overwhelmed by His great love for you demonstrated by the fact that He gave His life for you, then gave His life to you and now, at this very moment, lives His life through you.

An eight-week video study guide of this book is available through our ministry. The video series consists of eight 30-minute sessions in which I present an overview of each weekly study. The teachings were recorded with a small group in a home, making the series very personal and causing it to be an effective supplemental resource to accompany the study of this book in small groups. If you would like more information about the Grace Walk Experience Video Series, you may contact the Grace Walk Ministries office at **1-800-472-2311** *or order online at* **www.gracewalk.org**. *You will also find there many other audio and video resources I have written and recorded.*

Also by Steve McVey

GRACE AMAZING

If your Christian life seems as dry as dust and you're just going around in circles, maybe you're wandering in the wilderness. There, you feel as though…

- you live by the rules, and the Bible is the rule book
- you work hard for God…but you never quite measure up

But in the land of God's amazing grace, you experience the truth that…

- God has made you alive *in Christ*—and now you want to do what He wants
- Jesus has done all the work, and you can rest in the Father's acceptance

Steve McVey reveals more of the heart of your loving, giving Father…so you can better grasp just why His grace is so amazing.

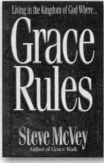

Living in the Kingdom of God Where…
GRACE RULES

Are you "living by the rules"…or are you letting God's grace rule you? There's a big difference. If you're living *for* God—living by the rules—you'll always be exhausted. You'll feel as if you're not doing enough for Him…and that if you don't "measure up," He'll be displeased with you.

But God never meant for you to live the Christian life that way! He sent Christ to set you free from rules. He didn't call you to serve Him in your own feeble power…but to let *His* limitless power flow through you! Find out how to rest in His grace and let Him live through you in *Grace Rules*.

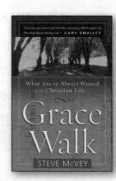

What You've Always Wanted in the Christian Life…
GRACE WALK

Nothing you have ever done, nothing you could ever do, will match the incomparable joy of letting Jesus live His life through you. It is what makes the fire of passion burn so brightly in new believers. And it is what causes the light of contentment to shine in the eyes of mature believers who have learned the secret of the *Grace Walk*.

If you know how to live it, you'll be strengthened by the depth of Steve McVey's insights. If you long for it, you can begin today!